THE FIX YOUR DEPRESSION HANDBOOK

Bringing you out of the darkness
and into a brilliant new world

FAUST RUGGIERO, M.S.

FYHB PUBLISHING

Disclaimer: The text that follows is designed to help you understand the dynamics of depression, and to provide some helpful steps to assist you in your attempts to reduce its impact on your life. Before attempting to incorporate the information and action steps in this book, consult a physician to be sure that you are physically, emotionally, an intellectually capable of including the program into your life.

Published by:
FYHB Publishing
BANGOR, PA
www.faustruggiero.com

Copyright © 2024 Faust A. Ruggiero

All rights reserved. No part of this publication may be reproduced, stored in a retrieval system, copied in any form or by any means, electronic, mechanical, photocopying, recording or otherwise transmitted without written permission from the publisher.

ISBNs:
Paperback: 978-1-7343830-4-1
Ebook: 978-1-7343830-5-8

Cover and interior design by Gary A. Rosenberg
www.thebookcouple.com

Printed in the United States of America

Literary Titan—Gold Award: 5 Stars • May 2, 2020

"*The Fix Yourself Handbook* by Faust Ruggiero is the key to being someone who can still move forward and find happiness, despite life changing events. This is a guide to being a better person and learning from your mistakes. A guide to getting up quickly after falling. A guide to truly living, as opposed to simply existing; stewing in our self-inflicted misery. Ruggiero understands that the steps to improving and becoming better need not be complex.

"*The Fix Yourself Handbook* is a book you would want to keep on hand to reference whenever you need guidance. I recommend this book to anyone who is looking for personal transformation through an easy to understand method."

—LITERARY TITAN • https://literarytitan.com/2020/04/27/

"*The Fix Yourself Handbook* is an action-filled plan for decreasing negativity, increasing joy, and embracing yourself. It presents a clear direction for an improved and enhanced life.

—JENNIFER NOLL FOR INDIEREADER BOOK REVIEWS

"The chapters are very well-structured; they follow a pattern that makes a wealth of information easy to understand and navigate. I felt that this is an actual handbook that readers can use as a reference, going back to it when facing challenges in life."

—ONLINEBOOKCLUB.ORG

"Faust Ruggiero's prose is bracingly clear and robust, and his insights into the normal crosscurrents of life are simultaneously simple common sense and powerfully innovative thinking about how his readers can sharpen and enhance their control over their own lives, balancing self-care with empathy. "Understand that you will never, ever please everyone all the time," he writes. "Make sure that whatever you choose to do is something you feel comfortable doing, and that it's the correct action to take." Readers will find these clarifications invaluable. A clear and intensely useful overview aimed at improving your life."

—THE KIRKUS REVIEW, MAY 4, 2020 • www.kirkusreviews.com/book-reviews/faust-ruggiero/the-fix-yourself-handbook/

"It is time to grab a copy of this book and get ready to be real with yourself. It has so much to explore and learn in the sections, but you cannot just read it and put it down. You will have to put in the mental work to get the best results. I am all about the power of positive thinking and trying to reach my best self every day, so this book is a great resource for strength, guidance and wisdom."

—CASSANDRA'S REVIEWS, FOR GOODREADS
www.goodreads.com/review/show/3260776759

PRAISE FOR FAUST RUGGIERO AND *THE FIX YOUR ANXIETY HANDBOOK*

"*The Fix Your Anxiety Handbook* demystifies the causes of anxiety and helps readers create an actionable plan in order to manage their anxiety. The step-by-step process is eye-opening and will help those suffering from this condition to understand the cause and work to heal. This self-help book is a valuable resource for everyone, whether they suffer from anxiety, have loved ones that do, or just want a better understanding of themselves and how to improve their mental health."

—5 STARS, LITERARY TITAN

What Readers Have Said about *THE FIX YOURSELF HANDBOOK*

SILVER WINNER,
Nonfiction Authors Association Book Awards

"*The Fix Yourself Handbook* offers an interesting range of approaches to becoming more objective and less emotional about life experiences in order to stay centered and peaceful. The formulas suggested can clearly be helpful for people who are working with counselors in therapy or recovery programs and also for readers seeking guidance to create more self-discipline."

—NONFICTION AUTHORS ASSOCIATION BOOK AWARDS

Readers' Favorite—Review Rating: 5 Stars

"The Fix Yourself Handbook: Using the Process Way of Life to Transform Your Life into a Happy, Healthy Journey by Faust Ruggiero is an insightful and profound book. It will motivate readers to make a healthy transformation in their lives by taking an inner journey and understanding how to use happiness and fulfillment there to find peace and love themselves. The author gives a step-by-step program, 'The Process Way of Life,' which is helpful when it comes to transforming life into one that is happy, healthy, purposeful, and contented.

"The Fix Yourself Handbook is uplifting and positive and gives hope to many readers who are stuck in patterns where their lives are not productive or happy. This book will guide readers on an enlightening and exciting journey that will touch every part of them. It gets them ready to begin a most wonderful journey. I like Faust Ruggiero's approach to a topic that is useful, and the methodical and well-structured discussion makes it easy for readers to comprehend and incorporate the suggestions into their daily lives. It is a good book to read to enhance personal growth and development in a positive way and make healthy transformations."

—MAMTA MADHAVAN FOR READERS' FAVORITE
https://readersfavorite.com/book-review/the-fix-yourself-handbook

"Faust Ruggiero has devised a unique psychological method by which anyone might find a better direction for coping with life's challenges."

—BARBARA BAMBERGER SCOTT, US REVIEW

Contents

Foreword..ix

Introduction 1

1. Dispelling the Myths: Getting the Real Story
   About Depression.. 10
2. The Faces of Depression: It's Not a One-Size-Fits-All......... 17
3. Signs and Symptoms: Proactivity as a Defensive Ally........... 23
4. The Body-to-Mind/Mind-to-Body Paradigm II:
   The Life-Changing Tag Team Duo 45
5. Disconnected: Understanding Who's Behind the Mask,
   and Why 51
6. Stuck in the Mud: Spinning Your Intellectual/Emotional
   Wheels 58
7. Leave Me Alone/Alone in the Crowd: Feeling Alone
   in the Darkness and What to Do About It..................... 66
8. Cousins in Crime: The Depression/Anxiety Relationship...... 74
9. My Personal Nemesis: Darkness with an Individual Touch.... 82
10. Not Giving In: Making the Decision to Get Healthy........... 89
11. Leaving the Past in the Past: Forgiveness and Learning
    to Feel Worthy.. 97
12. Putting Your Plan in Motion: It All Starts with Getting
    Your Body Healthy 106

13. Retraining Your Brain: Bringing Control Back to Your Intellectual Command Center..................................116

14. Action, Action! The Benefits of a Body in Motion............129

15. Starting Your Treatment Plan: Identifying Your Team and Letting Them In..136

16. To Medicate or Not to Medicate: Taking the Emotion out of an Important Decision...................................146

17. The Safe Place: Bringing Your Person into Your Life........159

18. Accepting Change: Out of the Darkness, One Little Step at a Time..167

19. Learning How Powerful You Can Be: Embracing "I Can"..175

20. Incremental and Consistent: The Step-by-Step Approach Explained..183

21. Learning to Live in Your New World: Applying Your Changes One Step at a Time...........................191

22. Defining Your New Personal Normal: Understanding That You Do Belong...197

23. Good Housekeeping: Keeping Order in Your New World..206

Conclusion..213

References..215

About the Author...217

Foreword

I HAVE KNOWN FAUST RUGGIERO SINCE AUGUST 2022 when he was a guest on my *Coast to Coast AM* radio program. I have been the host of *Coast to Coast AM* for over twenty years, and I have had the privilege of interviewing fascinating guests with much to offer. Mr. Ruggiero quickly stood out as one of those guests, as we discussed the topic of anxiety and *The Fix Your Anxiety Handbook*. He was asked to be a guest for a second time in August 2023, following the completion of *The Fix Your Depression Handbook*. Once again, it was an interesting interview with a very good response from the audience.

In our first interview, I found him to be personable, and his understanding of and ability to communicate the dynamics of anxiety quickly impressed me. He presented so much of the missing information about anxiety and also provided the audience with practical advice to help them understand their own anxiety and what they can do to obtain help for it. I was impressed with the smooth, easy approach he took to answering questions and as he communicated with my audience.

I took the time to read this book for which I am writing this foreword and was so impressed with the way the information was presented and how it effortlessly dispelled the myths about depression and presented factual information readers could use to establish their own personal treatment plan. Mr. Ruggiero presents depression as though it is a living monster who resides inside your body and mind. This helps people understand that they are fighting a condition that they have, rather than fighting themselves. As Mr.

Ruggiero states, "The most important point to understand is that depression is not who you are; it is what you have."

The chapters are short and to the point with information that is direct and concise. This book can also be used as a reference guide if you need it in the future. The layout makes it easy to refer to any chapter you might need a refresher on. In the "Time to Take Action" sections, you will have a clear understanding of the exact steps to take to help you alleviate the problem examined in that chapter. Depression can be a difficult condition to beat, but it is not impossible to do so when you have a process to follow.

With over four decades of counseling people with many issues, including anxiety and depression, Faust Ruggiero possesses an abundance of information and has created program to treat depression unlike any I have seen before. He has insights into the dynamics of depression and communicates them in a way anyone can understand and apply.

After all these years, Mr. Ruggiero still displays the love and respect that are so necessary in a world so in need of services like his. It is refreshing to see his level of commitment and willingness to remain in service of others. Not only is he acutely knowledgeable about his subject matter, but he is also a true humanitarian with an unbridled dedication to improve the human condition.

After spending time with him on two different occasions on my show, I am so impressed with his dedication and his level of expertise. *The Fix Your Depression Handbook* presents a program that can change your life.

—George Noory
Host of *Coast to Coast AM*

Introduction

DO YOU WANT TO UNDERSTAND DEPRESSION, reduce its impact on your life, and eventually free yourself from its paralyzing effects? If so, The *Fix Your Depression Handbook* is for you. This is book three in The Fix Yourself Empowerment Series. It follows the award-winning *The Fix Yourself Handbook,* which debuted in December 2019, and much heralded *The Fix Your Anxiety Handbook,* published in June, 2023.

Consistent with the approach taken in the first two volumes in the series, the program is presented as a process journey. All the books in The Fix Yourself Empowerment Series are written as journeys. I do this because I want you to understand that life is a journey, and by going slow and understanding the processes associated with it, you can learn how to live a happy and productive life. Also, by presenting the program as a life-journey, I can give you a glimpse of what your life can be like during the latter stages of the journey, that is, what your life can look like if you stay committed to what you are reading here. The most important point to remember is that depression is not who you are, it is what you have. I present depression as though it is a living monster, an actual beast that has invaded your mind and your body. You will see the term *life thief* used to describe the condition.

I describe depression this way to help you understand what is happening to your body, your mind, and your emotions. I want you to be able to separate yourself from the condition and to create a clearer picture of what has happened to you as depression becomes a dominant force in your life. When depression takes hold of your life, the pain it causes overwhelms you, making it difficult for you to understand what is happening to you. However, since depression is not who you are but what you have, treating it as such allows you to feel as though you are attacking something other than yourself—because you are.

Each bite-size chapter presents the necessary information you will need to understand a specific dynamic about the condition. The causes of your depression and how it exerts its influence are discussed, and the precise steps to help you correct the problem are provided as the chapters wind down. I have designed this program so you may apply the steps to your own personal circumstances as they exist in *your* life. However, as you will see, the problems presented here can be experienced by anyone who suffers from depression and is looking for a way out of their pain. You are not as different as you think you are, and there is a logical way out of your distress.

The Fix Your Depression Handbook is the product of more than thirty years of practical counseling application. I have developed the program, researched it extensively, and used it with great success with my clients. It is a dynamic addition to an existing counseling program, or, if you have difficulty obtaining professional counseling, it can provide you with either a viable alternative or an introduction to that step.

Each chapter in The Fix Yourself Empowerment Series opens with a quote that offers a glimpse into the chapter's content. This is followed by the specific processes to employ (See page XX), which will help you do the work to alleviate the problem addressed in the chapter. I have included the processes as program supports to help you work with all the information and suggestions I am making. The processes are nothing more than tools you can use as you attempt to implement each step of the program. As you proceed through the program and secure the assistance of counselor and support people to help you through your depression, these processes can be included in your discussions with them, and they will help you make the changes I will be discussing. A few processes—Brutal Honesty, I Over E, Present/Understand/Fix, and Slowing Down Life's Pace—appear in each chapter because they are foundational to the entire program.

There are fifty-two processes in the process way of life program. However, not all of them will directly apply to depression. The initial fifty-two processes were included in each chapter of *The Fix Yourself Handbook*, the program's flagship book. In that book, the text is written to address many different problems on the human spectrum, all fifty-two processes were needed to navigate through the program presented in the book. In the subsequent books, only the processes that directly apply to the information being discussed in the chapter will be used. So, don't be concerned if not all the processes are used in this particular book.

I have kept the chapters short and to the point, with information that is direct and concise. I have found this is the best way to ensure the information is understood, especially when depression so drastically reduces your ability to focus and concentrate. Since the book is also going to be used as a reference guide for you should you need it in the future, the design makes it easier to refer back to each chapter if you need to refresh yourself at a later date.

As the chapters conclude, you will find the Time to Take Action sections. Here, I present the exact steps I advise you to take to help alleviate the problem examined in the chapter. In everything I teach, I always provide action steps, because information without a workable course of action is rarely able to be applied. These action steps are the fuel that makes the program run. I have also provided you with a declaration at the end of each. These affirmations will help you maintain your enthusiasm as you continue to address the issues presented in the chapter. The chapter closes with a short introduction to what will be covered in the next chapter.

As you move forward in your life, it will be important for you to embrace the concept of information-gathering and fact-finding. Correct information always leads to the potential for a solution. With this in mind, Chapters 1 through 9 are designed to explain the dynamics of depression. It is vital to read these chapters carefully because they will provide you with the foundational information you need to create an efficient plan to address your depression.

Chapters 10 through 21 begin building your treatment plan to banish the depression—life thief—from your world. These chapters provide you with specific features of a workable plan to help alleviate your depression, as well as the steps you need to take to formulate that plan and begin your process of recovery from this debilitating nemesis.

Chapter 22 provides you with the information you need to live in the new world you are creating. Many people do their best to end their pain and move into a new way of life, but it can be difficult to stay there since they do not have an efficient plan to follow. This chapter provides you with the information to do just that. Chapter 23 provides a viable plan to help you maintain the gains you have made in your recovery from depression.

The book provides you with the initial tools to help you move beyond your depression, and will always be available as a reference guide and a lifelong support ally. Consistent with any program I design and implement, it is not meant to be a quick-fix problem-solver. This is a lifelong program designed to provide the information you need to help move you beyond your depression, and live a happy and healthy life free of the life thief.

If you are willing to give this program your time and commitment, it will become an invaluable part of your everyday life. You are greater than the depression that has been defining your life. In fact, you are great! So, get ready to become the master of your destiny. Prepare yourself for a life-changing program. There is a way out of your depression . . . and this is that way! Follow me.

HOW TO READ THIS BOOK

The Fix Your Depression Handbook and the program that supports it is a program for life, and nothing about it should ever move quickly. I advise that you read each chapter slowly, and before you move on to the next chapter, think about what you have read and how you can apply the information in the chapter. Move to the next chapter when you think you understand what you have read and repeat the process with that chapter.

For some of you, it may be important to read each chapter two or three times. Doing so can provide a better opportunity to understand the information the chapter provides. All of it is designed to provide you with what you need to define your depression, and to eventually work through it. It is a good idea to share what you are reading with people you are close with. If you already have a counselor, share it with that person also.

Depression can be a difficult condition to beat, but it is not impossible to do so. Take your time with the program, work the action steps as best as you can, and let others be there to counsel and support you as you take the steps to rid yourself of the depression life thief and live the happy life that has been waiting for you.

Since depression can have such a profound effect on your motivation to carry out tasks, and your brain's ability to understand what you are reading, it's a good idea to share this book with a close friend who can help you understand and interpret the information you are reading.

NOTE: the sole purpose of the information in this book is presented to help you understand the dynamics of depression, and to suggest some healthy alternatives to help you begin a program that can assist you alleviate your depression. Before starting any program, consult your physician to determine if there is any reason to avoid it, or if changes in your medical program need to be addressed before you start.

THE PROCESSES—CATEGORIES AND DESCRIPTIONS

	Process	Description
1	**Personal Inventory** (Alternate and/or related terms: *Internal Focus, Morality*)	The process of focusing our energy inward to allow for the identification of personal strengths and self-understanding, with the goal of understanding our personal principles concerning the distinction between right and wrong.
2	**Slow and Steady** (Alternate and/or related terms: *Patience, Slowing Down Life's Pace, Incremental Forward Movement*)	The movement away from quick and impulsive behaviors, and into a state of willful tolerance of delay through the deceleration of a lifestyle that leads to poor decisions and internal conflict, with the understanding that only through small, well-planned steps can we create sustained change and improve the quality of our lives.
3	**Honesty** (Alternate and/or related terms: *Brutal Honesty, Humility, Truth-Telling*)	The process of being absolutely honest with ourselves, even to the point of personal discomfort, and choosing to take a modest view of our own importance for the purposes of opening oneself up to personal growth.
4	**I Over E** (Intellect over Emotion) (Alternate and/or related terms: *Emotional Control, Fact-Finding, Intelligent Decision-Making*)	Taking the steps necessary to reduce the impact of emotions on our intellectual processes and using our intellect to exhaustively search for the facts in situations that may lead to stress and personal problems, before our emotions have an opportunity to distort them. Cultivating the understanding that knowledge must be applied so it may become a parameter of personal growth.
5	**Present-Understand-Fix** (Alternate and/or related terms: *Fact-Finding*)	The formula we will use in every chapter to address your problems. We present the problem, we use the facts to understand it, and we take the steps to fix it.

6	**Surrendering to the Process** (Alternate and/or related terms: Trust, Faith, Belief, Honor, Dignity)	The willingness to have unconditional trust, either in a process or some unknown entity, such as a higher power, and to allow ourselves to become subservient to the processes, so that we can learn to believe in ourselves, knowing we are capable of being the person we want to be. Having learned to do this, we can learn to think, feel, and behave in a fashion that raises our consciousness to higher-order thoughts and feelings and connects us to our innermost spirit.
7	**Effective Communication** (Alternate and/or related terms: Warm Confrontation, Positive Language Reciprocity, Communication, Conflict Resolution, Listening)	Understanding and mastering the art of positive information exchanges. The ability to gather the facts, understand them, place them in an internally cohesive framework and present that framework, intelligently, to others to address problems. Learning to listen to ourselves, and to others, even if the information presents challenges. Understanding that the way we speak to ourselves and to others can set the stage for how we feel about ourselves and how we communicate with others.
8	**Cleaning House** (Alternate and/or related terms: Life Inventory, Eliminating Toxic People, Housekeeping, Gatekeeping, Boundary-Setting)	The honest review of one's life and those relationships in it. The removal of all people, events, and situations that may cause pain, conflict, confusion, or dysfunction from one's life to make way for positive and functional information and life-enhancing processes, followed by the practice of monitoring who and what may enter our lives thereafter. Setting boundaries regarding who gets in and how close, and learning to defend those boundaries.
9	**Simplifying Life** (Alternate and/or related terms: Life on Life's Terms, Keeping Life Simple, Life's Natural Flow)	Understanding how to apply life's natural flow in our lives, along with the removal of any irrational, unreasonable expectations, and unnecessary complexity from life to make room for a simpler and more productive way of living.

10	**Living the Journey** (Alternate and/or related terms: Reduction of Destination Living, One-Day-at-a-Time Living, Living in the Moment, Journey Living, Creativity, Passion, Humor)	Releasing one's attachment to a happiness in life that is dependent on one's arrival at specific, magnificent destinations in favor of focusing on the present, with minimum movement back to past people and events, or forward to events which have not yet occurred. The willingness to focus all life energy on our present life and happiness, moment by moment, as life is being lived, and to appreciate the lighter sides of life, thus reducing stress and pain.
11	**Closure on the Past** (Alternate and/or related terms: *Settling Past Issues, Forgiveness*)	Judiciously reviewing all past situations and events to put closure on them. Once we've done this, we undertake a step-by-step process to understand what we and others have done wrong, to make amends, and allow ourselves to move forward with reduced emotional pain; forgiving ourselves and others who may have hurt us.
12	**Eyes on the Prize** (Alternate and/or related terms: *Goal-Setting, Time/Energy Management, Learning to Be Comfortable with Being Uncomfortable, Risk-Taking*)	The practice of setting a long-term goal, complete with short-term goals, action steps, and an executable plan to carry them out in a coherent, cohesive, and timely fashion, and then consciously managing our daily clock and applying our energy to healthy modes of thought and behavior. Change, by definition, is unsettling. Temporary, uncomfortable time frames lead to the happiness and fulfillment we seek. That is where understanding and growth live.
13	**Commitment** (Alternate and/or related terms: *Journey Living, Trust, Faith*)	Enduring dedication. The Process Way of Life takes time, and continuous, unwavering commitment to the program is essential to ensure its success.
14	**Service** (Alternate and/or related terms: *Being in Service*)	The willingness to turn our rewards outward to help serve the needs of others without expectation of notoriety or payback.

15	**Wisdom** (Alternate and/or related terms: *Sustained Learning, Humility*)	Being committed to remaining an eternal student of life's lessons and positive teaching sources so we can reach our goal of having the experience, knowledge, and good judgment to achieve an understanding of the bigger picture in life and how to apply ourselves there.
16	**Gratitude** (Alternate and/or related terms: *Trust, Faith, Belief, Honor, Dignity*)	The understanding that we must be grateful for all we are, all we have, and all we can be, and that we must express this in every moment of our lives.
17	**Maintaining the Program** (Alternate and/or related terms: *System Maintenance, Housekeeping*)	The establishment and maintenance of an internally balanced power source where the intellect, emotions, body, and spirit become one. This power source is always alive and functional, emanating from inside ourselves.
18	**Internal Balance**	This is the goal of the program. It is the point where our physical, intellectual, emotional, and spiritual attributes operate in a state of enhanced equilibrium.
19	**Pure Love**	That point in the Process Way of Life where, through internal balance, we allow our new power source to be realized, to wrap itself around all we feel, touch, see, and do. This is love at its purest level.

CHAPTER 1

Dispelling the Myths: Getting the Real Story About Depression

Dispelling the Myths—The Truth About Depression is never built on myths and misdirection. Know the facts before you move forward.

PROCESSES TO EMPLOY: Brutal Honesty, I Over E, Present/Understand/Fix, Slowing Down Life's Pace, Internal Focus, Fact-Finding

IT COMES LIKE A THIEF IN THE NIGHT, stealing pieces of your mind, wrecking your emotions, and making off with the most precious parts of your life. Nothing rocks the human spirit like depression. Clinical depression is a mental health disorder characterized by persistently depressed mood or loss of interest in activities, causing significant impairment in daily life. It can reduce even the most sophisticated minds to an unmotivated and disconnected way of living. People who suffer from depression experience an intellectual, emotional, and physical disconnection, and report difficulties performing even the simplest of tasks.

The causes of depression can include a combination of biological, psychological, and social sources of distress. Increasingly, research suggests these factors may cause changes in brain function, including altered activity of certain neural circuits in the brain. Since the brain and its neurological pathways need these neural circuits to operate efficiently, the reduction in their ability to perform can have a profound effect on the way people think, feel, and behave.

The persistent feeling of sadness or loss of interest that characterizes major depression can lead to a range of behavioral and physical symptoms. These may include changes in sleep, appetite, energy level, concentration, daily behavior, and self-esteem. Depression can also be associated with thoughts of suicide.

Clinical depression (also known as major depression, or major depressive disorder) is a common but serious mood disorder. It causes severe symptoms that affect how a person feels, thinks, and handles daily activities, such as sleeping, eating, socializing, working, and relating to others. Typically, to be diagnosed with depression, the symptoms must be present for at least two consecutive weeks.

THE REAL AND THE NOT-SO-REAL

There are so many myths about this life stealing condition. I will start by separating fact from fiction.

FICTION: Depression isn't a real illness.
FACT: Depression is indeed classified as a real illness. It alters the chemistry of the brain, and neurologically it can affect every system in the body.

FICTION: Antidepressants cure depression.
FACT: Antidepressants do not provide an absolute cure for depression. They can, however, help reduce the physical symptoms, as well as provide some neurological balance, and they may be a good first step to begin addressing depression.

FICTION: You can snap out of it on your own.
FACT: Since depression affects the brain's ability to interpret information and act upon it, making a decision to simply stop its effects on the body and the brain is rarely possible.

FICTION: Depression occurs as the result of a sad situation.

FACT: Difficult situations do not cause depression. There may be a short-lived period in which the brain needs to adjust to an emotional or environmental trauma, but someone without depression should have no problem eventually working through the event. On the other hand, people who do suffer from depression, even lighter cases of depression, may become more depressed as a result of a triggering event.

FICTION: If one or both of your parents had/have depression, so will you.

FACT: Where there are genetic factors involved in depression, you don't simply become depressed because your parents had the problem. Neurologically, one can be genetically predisposed, but that does not necessarily mean that the condition will develop and become serious simply because of genetics.

FICTION: Antidepressants change your personality.

FACT: Antidepressants do not change personality. There are times when they are overprescribed, or there may be other drug interactions, and a person's personality seems to be different. Antidepressants are designed to simply stimulate the brain to do what it is neurologically designed to do. If you feel that your personality has changed, and you do not like the change, do consult your physician.

FICTION: You will have to be on antidepressants forever.

FACT: This is not always true. For some individuals diagnosed with major depression, antidepressants may be part of the long-term treatment plan. Typically, they can be a good way to start treatment, but they should always be part of a counseling program that teaches both coping skills and alternative ways to live that can successfully address your depression.

FICTION: Depression primarily affects women.

FACT: This is absolutely not true. Men are just as likely to become depressed as women, but often men will express their depression differently. For example, they may become more aggressive and/or angrier. However, like their female counterparts, they may experience mild to severe effects physically, emotionally, and intellectually, Depression does not discriminate.

FICTION: Talking about your fears, worries, and feelings makes it worse.

FACT: Part of the difficulty associated with depression is not being able to communicate one's feelings and other concerns as a result of diminished cognitive capacity. However, counseling and talking through the depression and its triggering events is one of the most efficient ways to combat this menacing life thief.

FICTION: Depression is always triggered by adversity or life transitions.

FACT: This is not necessarily true. For some people, the change in the body's chemical reactions can trigger depressive episodes. For others, there are life events that can act as triggers, and people suffering from depression may see increased depressive symptoms. So, where personal and environmental triggers can have an impact on depression, they are not necessary for depressive episodes to occur.

FICTION: Depression is only a mental problem.

FACT: Depression is primarily a physical problem and the result of neurotransmitter imbalance that affects the brain. We will discuss more about this in Chapter 4.

FICTION: Depression is a sign of weakness.

FACT: Depression is by no means a sign of weakness, even though it can become debilitating enough to make one feel as though they are weak. It takes considerable strength to fight the condition, and with help, the symptoms can be sharply reduced and, at times, completely eliminated.

FICTION: Hard work beats depression.

FACT: Recovery is not only about hard work. In fact, it is difficult to motivate oneself to do hard work when depression is ruling one's life. It takes doing hard work in the right way to bring you through your depression This is why getting help is so important.

FICTION: Depression is just self-pity.

FACT: It is very easy to get down on yourself when depression rules your life. People can get lost in depressive thoughts and feelings of low self-worth and low self-esteem. These, however, are the result of depression: and do not cause it. Again, communicating about it can be the beginning of a plan to successfully address your depression.

FICTION: Depressed people cry a lot.

FACT: Emotional expressions can be a part of depression. However, very often, depressed people have a difficult time expressing emotions, including crying. Sometimes, depression can seem to turn on a dime, and all of a sudden you feel emotional. Crying, however, is usually more consistent with the way people typically express themselves. People who are generally more emotionally expressive will cry more often when they are depressed.

FICTION: You can never really beat depression.

FACT: The combination of medication, alternative medical procedures, counseling, and a good support network can provide a person who is willing to do the work with, at the very least, a moderate to significant reduction of their depressive symptomology.

Becoming Your Own Expert

All too often, with depression or any other illness, people experiencing the problem have not done the necessary research to understand the problem. You need to do as much fact-finding as you can to increase your understanding of the problem you are experiencing and, to some extent, what you personally can do about it.

Medicine tends to come into play too fast in today's accelerated, quick-fix way of doing things. This can leave you at the hands of a system that does not provide you with the facts you need, and can often deliver less than efficient treatments for what is affecting you. Your first step in combating this merciless life thief is to understand everything you can about what depression can do to you physically, intellectually, emotionally, and even spiritually. As we go more in depth, you will see that this is, in fact, a condition that is stealing your life from you, and the most important thing you can do is to become your own depression expert. This paves the way for the new life that can be yours with a treatment program based on knowledge and efficient treatment planning.

 TIME TO TAKE ACTION

1. Seek as much accurate information about depression as you can. Do an internet study. Listen to podcasts and any other information sources that can increase your knowledge base with respect to the dynamics of depression.

2. Make an appointment with your primary care physician. Talk to them about what you are experiencing, and ask to have your blood tested to determine if there are any other underlying physical factors that are either causing or exacerbating your symptoms.

3. If you are willing, make an appointment for a consultation with a psychologist or a professional counselor. Make sure this person has an expertise in the diagnosis and treatment of depression. You do not have to continue the counseling if you don't want to, but making this appointment will help you acquire more information a familiarize you with someone who may be part of your treatment plan as you go forward.

 **DRIVING IT HOME**

Depression is indeed a life thief. It can seriously affect the way you think, feel, and behave. It can impact every part of your life, including your relationships and your employment. It can keep you isolated from some of the most important people and events in your life. Creating a treatment plan that can help you defeat the depression life thief starts with acquiring the knowledge you need to understand what is happening to your body and your mind. It is an important first step in beginning to take back your life and help you become the happy person you were meant to be.

YOUR DECLARATION IS: *I will arm myself with the information I need to beat the life thief, and I will take back my life!*

 **ONWARD**

Arming yourself with the information you need to beat the life thief opens the door to everything you need to become a happy person. In the next chapter, I'll show you the different faces of depression. Not everyone's depression is the same, and it is important to understand what yours looks like.

CHAPTER 2

The Faces of Depression: It's Not a One-Size-Fits-All

Depression has many faces. Getting to know yours is instrumental in moving beyond the clutches of this life thief.

PROCESSES TO EMPLOY: Brutal Honesty, I Over E, Present/Understand/Fix, Slowing Down Life's Pace, Internal Focus, Fact-Finding

IN ANY HUMAN EXPERIENCE, THERE ARE THE universal characteristics of that experience, and there are subjective characteristics specific to the individual. This applies to all the good things we experience, and also to those more challenging situations and events in our lives. Anyone can experience depression, and if you do, some of the symptoms you will experience will be generalized. This means they will be experienced by most anyone who has depression. For some of the symptoms, however, the way you respond to them physically, emotionally, and intellectually will be specific to you. Your depression, in this sense, is yours and yours alone.

THE FACE YOU WEAR

There are many different types of depression, and it is important for you to understand how to differentiate between the types of depression, and the symptoms that pertain to each. Though you may suffer from a specific type of depression, the different types do share symptomology that, at times, makes it difficult to know which type you are experiencing. A basic understanding regarding the different types of depression and how they affect you, which I will establish in this chapter, will be invaluable when you arrive at Chapter 10, where I will begin to discuss how to treat this nefarious affliction.

I am going to start by presenting the different types of depression. It is important for you to understand what causes the varying types of depression, how they manifest themselves, and, eventually, the treatment for each.

I will outline the more prevalent types of depression. Do not diagnose yourself based on these definitions. They are simply intended to help you understand what depression is and how it may relate to what you are experiencing. Consult a physician or a professional counselor if you feel the information provided here describes what you are feeling in your life. I am simply listing them here. In Chapter 3, I will expand on the symptoms described in this chapter to help you gain a clearer perspective regarding your experience with depression.

- **MAJOR DEPRESSION**—Major or clinical depression symptoms usually last at least two weeks and include depressed mood or loss of interest that interferes with daily activities. There is often little interest or pleasure in activities, feeling down, depressed, or hopeless, trouble falling or staying asleep, or sleeping too much, feeling tired or having little energy, poor appetite, overeating, or considerable weight changes, feeling bad about yourself, thoughts of failure or guilt, difficulty concentrating on things or making decisions, and suicidal thoughts.

- **DYSTHYMIA, OR LOW-GRADE DEPRESSION**—Also known as persistent depressive disorder, dysthymia symptoms are present almost daily, and for years at a time. Dysthymia symptoms won't always stop you from functioning, but they will likely keep you from thriving and living your fullest life. The symptoms of low-grade depression include feelings of sadness, loss of interest in activities, feelings of worthlessness and hopelessness, low self-esteem, difficulty focusing, short-term memory problems, insomnia, and thoughts of self-harm. A persistent depressive disorder, the symptoms may vary in severity, but they usually do not subside for more than two months at a time.

- **SEASONAL AFFECTIVE DISORDER**—This is depression that fluctuates with the seasons, with symptoms typically worsening in the late fall and early winter and lessening during the spring and summer. People who have seasonal affective disorder can experience many of the symptoms in both major depression and dysthymia, but the symptoms tend to worsen during the months of the year where people are deprived of sunlight and when they spend more time indoors.

- **BIPOLAR DISORDER**—People with bipolar disorder (formerly called manic depression or manic-depressive illness) also experience depressive episodes during which they feel sad, indifferent, or hopeless, combined with a very low activity level. However, a person with bipolar disorder also experiences manic episodes, or unusually elevated moods in which they might feel very happy, irritable, or "up" with a marked increase in activity level.

- **PERINATAL DEPRESSION**—This form of depression occurs during or after pregnancy. Depression that begins during pregnancy is prenatal depression, and depression that begins after the baby is born is postpartum depression. A woman's body undergoes significant hormonal changes during pregnancy, and those hormonal changes can continue after the baby is born. The condition can be particularly difficult if the woman has a history of mental health problems, particularly depression earlier in life, or a history of mental health problems during pregnancy, few close family or friends for support, or relationship difficulties. Perinatal depression can be experienced for a short period of time, or it may persist for several years. It is often characterized by poor motivation, feelings of hopelessness, difficulty focusing and concentrating, and a general withdrawal from family and social events. In its most severe presentation, the mother will consider leaving her situation or, at times, ending her life.

➢ **DEPRESSION WITH SYMPTOMS OF PSYCHOSIS**—This is a severe form of depression in which a person experiences psychotic symptoms, such as delusions (disturbing, false fixed beliefs) or hallucinations (hearing or seeing things others do not hear or see). This does not mean that people who experience delusions or hallucinations are psychotic. It means that when the brain is not processing information correctly, some of the symptoms resemble those of a person dealing with some level of psychosis. Since the brain is not receiving the neurotransmitters it needs to function properly, it can misperceive information or believe something that is not necessarily true, and at times, the person can become aggressive and combative.

RESPOND, DON'T REACT

One of the most important points to understand about depression is that it alters the way we perceive information. Depression is primarily a physical condition, the basis of which is a depletion of the neurotransmitters serotonin, norepinephrine, or dopamine in the central nervous system. Without going into a complex definition of human neurology, suffice it to say that when your brain is depressed, it is not receiving the neurotransmitters it needs to operate efficiently which causes you to misperceive information.

Depression makes it very difficult to perceive information correctly, let alone act on it efficiently, which is partly why I advise you to consult a physician or a counselor if you are suffering from the symptoms of depression. The brain needs a balanced supply of neurotransmitters to perform its daily activities efficiently. If you have depression, that is not happening. Learning all you can about depression can help you move forward toward effective treatment which will hopefully banish the life thief from your world.

I will discuss the physical effects of depression on your body, emotions, and brain in Chapter 4. For now, focus on getting the facts about depression. It is important to understand the defining terminology, the different kinds of depression and how they can affect you, the general symptoms of depression, and how depression affects the various systems of your body. You will need this information to help you build a treatment plan to reduce depression's impact on your life and help you become the happy productive person you want to be.

 TIME TO TAKE ACTION

1. In this first part of the program, your only goal should be to familiarize yourself with the language related to depression, the various types of depression, and the general symptoms. Do not try to fix anything now. Just take some time and expand your information base. Do some internet searches on the different types of depression. Be as informed as you can in these early stages.

2. If you feel you have depression, and may have identified one or more of the different types of depression affecting you, try not to be discouraged. The first step in working with any condition that affects you is defining its parameters. Sometimes, once we are certain we have a problem, we become overwhelmed and overly concerned with fixing it quickly. Getting the information is the first step in arriving at the diagnosis that will eventually lead to your solution. Your goal is to fix it correctly.

3. Begin to identify those professionals who can help you. As I mentioned in the action steps in Chapter 1, your primary care physician should be your first call. Also, begin taking the initial steps to identify a professional counselor. If you know someone who is seeing one, they might be able to provide you with either a source for counseling or, at the very least, some actionable steps to help you find a counselor who can assist you in the future.

4. If you feel you are depressed, reach out to someone who can support you. Nothing positive happens with depression when you're all alone. As we proceed, I am going to be talking more about your primary care physician, acquiring a counselor to help you, and your support network. All will be so important in your movement away from the life thief.

 DRIVING IT HOME

Nothing about depression feels good. Having your life stolen from you is painful, and it can cause you to feel hopeless. Try to be patient. I have counseled people with depression for over four decades, and I know how to help you move forward. So for now, let's just focus on getting you the information you need to define what your next step is going to be. In this part of the program, I am simply helping you establish a good foundation, one we are going to use to help you get your life back.

YOUR DECLARATION IS: *I will define my depression, and I will do what it takes to be happy.*

 ONWARD

As you are beginning to understand what depression is, the various types of depression, and which one(s) may be affecting your life, our next step is to acquire the information necessary to define your particular symptoms. In the next chapter, I am going to expand on the signs and symptoms of the different types of depression I outlined in this chapter. This will prepare the stage for the changes you will need to make in the more advanced stages of the program.

CHAPTER 3

Signs and Symptoms: Proactivity as a Defensive Ally

The life thief lets you know it's coming. Learn to recognize its knock before you open the door.

PROCESSES TO EMPLOY: Brutal Honesty, I Over E, Present/Understand/Fix, Slowing Down Life's Pace, Internal Focus, Fact-Finding

THE OLD ADAGE IT'S DIFFICULT TO SEE the forest for the trees usually refers to the difficulties we may have seeing the bigger picture when that more extensive view is obscured and, at times, too much for us to comprehend. In terms of depression, it is difficult to understand what type of depression you have or to identify the symptoms—those changes in your thoughts, feelings, and behaviors—while they are overwhelming your life.

Since the physical changes in the brain can cause you to misperceive information, what you think you see may not always reflect reality. It is also hard to understand what you are thinking and feeling while you are in those depressive moments. That is because pain creates yet one more roadblock in your mind's ability to produce clarity of thought. Depression interferes with your ability to not only compile information, but also to place it in a coherent perspective, and make decisions based on that information. The effect on the much needed reciprocal relationship between your body and your mind is so drastically affected, that physically and intellectually, your resources to understand what is happening, and to make intelligent life choices are severely compromised.

This is why it is so difficult to attack the depression monster on your own. You will need help, and you will need accurate information. What follows is a discussion of the symptomatology of the different types of depression. I will explore the symptoms of each type of depression presented in Chapter 2, and help you understand what those symptoms look like. You will notice that there is some overlap in the symptoms. As I mentioned in Chapter 1, there are generalized attributes of depression, those symptoms everyone experiences, but there are also symptoms that may pertain just to your specific type of depression, and how you experience it.

The goal in this chapter is to simply help you understand the symptoms. Sometimes, symptom lists do not provide enough information about how those symptoms present, so they can be difficult to understand. That is why I am expanding on each of the symptoms. Again, stay away from diagnosing yourself. You are in the information-gathering stage, and I will help you understand what to do with the information as we proceed.

Try not to be concerned if the symptoms you are experiencing are listed in several of the sections. This is to be expected since many of the symptoms can present in each type of depression. You will learn more about what to do with it as we proceed.

TYPES OF DEPRESSION AND THEIR SYMPTOMS

Major Depression (Clinical Depression)

This is a mental health disorder characterized by persistently depressed mood or loss of interest in activities, causing significant impairment in daily life.

DEPRESSED MOOD OR LOSS OF INTEREST USUALLY LASTING FOR AT LEAST TWO WEEKS THAT INTERFERES WITH DAILY ACTIVITIES:

Everyone can get down just a bit, but usually people without depression bounce back returning to normal activities in two or three days. Major depression does not allow this, and this cycle can easily last for two weeks and, for some, far beyond.

LITTLE INTEREST OR PLEASURE IN DOING THINGS: Since depression causes a significant loss of energy, concentration, and focus, it is difficult to maintain interest in even the simplest of tasks.

DIFFICULTY CONCENTRATING OR MAKING DECISIONS: The ability to intellectually stay on point and to concentrate on what you need to do is severely compromised when your brain is feeling the effects of depression. Decision making is closely tied to the human ability to collect, organize, and interpret facts, and these skills are drastically reduced when the mind is depressed. As a result, your memory is affected, your ability to focus and concentrate is reduced, and you have a very difficult time making decisions.

PROCRASTINATION: Even when the brain is experiencing the effects of major depression, it does understand the need, and often the desire, to get things done. As a result, people with depression will say they are going to do something a little later, and they may even make a note to themselves that they need to get it done, but the lack of focus and energy can make it feel like an insurmountable task.

FEELING DOWN, DEPRESSED, OR HOPELESS: The human ability to feel pleasure and to enjoy life is tied very closely to the neurotransmitter chemicals our bodies produce. When the brain becomes clinically depressed and those chemicals are either absent, or not produced at levels that provide enough stimulation for the brain, any movement toward happiness is significantly reduced, and you will feel down, depressed, and often hopeless. The feeling of hopelessness is usually the product of repeated attempts to reduce depression with no success.

TROUBLE FALLING OR STAYING ASLEEP, OR SLEEPING TOO MUCH: For your brain to operate properly, it needs to efficiently fall asleep and stay asleep. Depression interferes with the brain's ability to sleep, and lack of sleep is very closely tied to imbalance in chemical production in the body and, ultimately, to your ability to be happy. Not sleeping well can have a profound effect on the way you feel. Cellular regeneration also occurs during deep sleep, and this is, all too often, compromised by difficulty sleeping.

FEELING TIRED OR HAVING LITTLE ENERGY: We often associate our ability to energize ourselves with the way our body performs and how we nurture our body to become energized. Keep in mind that the brain is part of the body, and it plays a significant part in controlling the energy production in the body. When you have depression, your body's ability to energize itself can be significantly affected.

POOR APPETITE, OVEREATING, OR CONSIDERABLE WEIGHT CHANGES: By now, you have probably heard that hunger and the feeling of satisfaction or fullness when you eat is not felt in your stomach, but rather in your brain. The brain controls appetite, what you like and don't like to eat, and your desire to eat. When your brain is operating in a depressed mode, your appetite will be affected. As a result, you will look for foods that make you feel good. Those pleasure foods, sadly, are usually the foods that have a negative impact on your health, your weight, and the way your brain operates.

FEELING BAD ABOUT YOURSELF: When you have a difficult time performing daily routines, being accountable to yourself and others, and even doing the simplest of chores, you begin to look at yourself as someone who is worthless, and you just might stay that way. This is two-pronged attack on your brain. First, you cannot do all the things you typically would, so you will feel bad about that. Then you start to believe you have nothing to offer, which has a profound effect on the way you feel about yourself. Also, your ability to feel good about yourself is based on the neurotransmitters that your brain is receiving, in balance. It is hard to feel good about yourself when your brain cannot make it happen.

THOUGHTS OF FAILURE OR GUILT AND SHAME: As the feelings about yourself continue to worsen, you may perceive yourself as a failure, and now feelings of failure, guilt, and shame take over your world. This is where your internal language changes, and your self-talk can range from mildly depressed to downright abusive. This is also when you feel the strong need to avoid other people.

SUICIDAL THOUGHTS: As feelings of worthlessness continue and you perceive that there is no way out of the horrors that now define your life, you may begin to think that you and the world around you would be better off if you were no longer in it. This is why it is so important to open up about your depression and to begin to construct a team of people and professionals who will be there for you and can help you change what is happening to your brain.

Dysthymia or Low-Grade Depression

This type of depression is characterized by symptoms that are persistent, not as severe as clinical depression, and usually last for at least two years.

FEELINGS OF SADNESS: The feelings of sadness that accompany dysthymia not as severe as those felt by people with clinical depression. Known as low-grade depression, it has many of the symptoms of its clinical counterpart, but they are less severe and though you may feel sad, you do possess the ability to work through the sadness.

LOSS OF INTEREST IN ACTIVITIES: People suffering from dysthymia often maintain their interest in their activities; however, they will experience a short-term reduction in the interest in the activities and will report that they are not experiencing the joy they thought they would experience while they were involved in those activities.

FEELINGS OF WORTHLESSNESS AND HOPELESSNESS: Low-grade depression can cause feelings of worthlessness and hopelessness. However, they are not as intense and typically do not last as long as clinical depression. Also, people with low-grade depression can experience gaps between depressive periods, but do possess the understanding that there may be a way out of it. They are also more prone to asking for help than their clinically depressed counterparts.

LOW SELF-ESTEEM: Every type of depression can produce low self-esteem. Someone suffering from depression, even low-grade depression, can also suffer from performance issues. Also, as with any type of depression, the brain is simply not receiving the neurotransmitters it needs when it needs them and in the proper balance. It is hard to feel good about yourself when there seems to be a force-field around your brain, and nothing good seems to get in or out.

DIFFICULTY FOCUSING: Anything that affects the way your brain functions is going to affect your ability to focus. Though depression is not a drug, it interferes with the way your brain works, just like drugs do. People I have counseled often say that when they are depressed, they feel as though they have taken too much medication, and they cannot seem to focus on what they are doing. In short, depression will always produce focusing and concentration issues.

SHORT-TERM MEMORY PROBLEMS: Memory is a function of a neurological coding and decoding process. Specifically, when your senses detect something, your brain needs to code it in order to commit it to memory. This means that it will stamp it with a neurological code and store it appropriately in your brain. When you would like to recall that memory, the brain's function is to decode it and present it in a fashion that closely resembles what you saw, heard, etc. Though in depression there is an adverse effect on the recall of the memory, the real issue is that the brain does not code the stimuli correctly, so when you attempt to recall it, you feel like it is not there, or it is fragmented and poorly represented. Again, depression interferes with both your brain's coding and the decoding (the recall) process.

INSOMNIA AND OTHER SLEEP DISORDERS: Even though dysthymia is a lower grade depression, it is still depression. It has the power to affect your ability to fall asleep and stay asleep. People who have depression also tend to keep dubious life schedules. They do not always do the same things at the same time. For most people, sleep requires a consistent schedule where the body rises at a certain time and retires at a certain time. This helps to facilitate the chemicals the body produces to fall asleep and stay there. Depressed people have a tendency to have inconsistent schedules, tend to stay up deep into the night, and sleep late in the morning. They will also take naps during the day that interfere with their ability to fall asleep at night. This does not always work well for the body, especially as it relates to healthy sleep patterns.

THOUGHTS OF SELF-HARM: Any form of depression can stimulate thoughts of self-harm. Most people with low-grade depression do not purposefully hurt themselves intentionally want to end their lives. The thought, however, may arise from time to time. The danger is that a triggering event could push the thoughts closer to a course of action. Since people suffering from low-grade depression are typically more communicative, it is always a good idea to discuss what you are feeling with others.

Seasonal Affective Disorder

People who have seasonal affective disorder often experience many of the symptoms found in both major depression and dysthymia, but the symptoms tend to worsen during the months of the year where people are deprived of sunlight and spend more time indoors.

ANXIETY: People tend to treat anxiety and depression as though they are completely different conditions. Though they do affect the body differently and are often displayed differently, they are closely related. When you are depressed and not receiving proper neurochemical uptake, you may move back and forth between periods of sadness and feeling anxious. Seasonal affective disorder tends to include both anxious and depressed periods in its presentation. I will be talking more about the relationship between anxiety and depression in Chapter 8.

APATHY: Depression almost always includes some form of apathy. If you are not apathetic, you are, at the very least, less interested than usual in activities and outcomes. People who suffer from seasonal affective disorder typically suffer from low-grade depression. So, the symptoms in the above section about dysthymia can also apply to seasonal affective disorder, but they will be exaggerated as a result of vitamin D deprivation, reduced activity, and "cabin fever."

GENERAL DISCONTENT: Most people suffering from seasonal affective disorder live in areas where they experience seasonal changes. In late fall until early spring when the sunlight is not direct and often seems to be absent, chemical production in the body changes. There are fewer opportunities to be active, and people's diet and sleep pattern changes. For them, it is difficult to feel content when the physical world has "gone dark" and so have their feelings.

LONELINESS: Loneliness usually enters the life of a person with seasonal affective disorder as the months progress. Initially, the change is subtle, but as the weeks wear on and as their neurology experiences changes, they begin to isolate, to participate in fewer social activities, and to feel lonely.

LOSS OF INTEREST: Though people with seasonal affective disorder tend to complain about having nothing to do, they often do not seek to do much. They tend to complain more, and they look at the world with depressed eyes. Social media, television, and other simple activities replace those that require more energy and engagement, and they may even turn down suggested activities because they are simply is not interested in doing anything different or they are too tired.

MOOD SWINGS OR SADNESS: Seasonal affective disorder does not produce the same type of depression every day. There are times when a person's mood may swing from a bit happy to sad to angry to depressed. Remember, this is low-grade depression experienced with a bit more push during a shorter segment of time. Unlike low-grade depression, which is present most of the time, a person with seasonal affective disorder will have moods that fluctuate, sometimes as a function of what is happening during their day, and other times with no apparent trigger.

EXCESSIVE TIREDNESS: The lack of activity that usually accompanies seasonal affective disorder often produces periods of extreme tiredness, with people reporting that all they want to do is lie down and take naps. Seasonal affective disorder can produce a type of lethargy that makes small periods of escape attractive and often difficult to stop.

INSOMNIA: Seasonal affective disorder, though it is often a temporary condition, is still a form of depression, and along with it comes difficulty in maintaining healthy sleep patterns. Again, just as with the other types of depression, the lack of sleep can give way to mood swings, loss of interest, apathy, etc. During the seasonal affective disorder time frame, people's sleep schedules will fluctuate, and this can also create difficult sleep experiences.

APPETITE CHANGES AND OR WEIGHT FLUCTUATIONS: Many forms of depression carry with them the perceived need for comfort foods, which are consumed in larger amounts and at inappropriate times. As a result, we see appetite changes and weight fluctuations during the times when people are closed in. It is often a coping device people use to try to feel better in these short-lived but difficult periods of depression.

FATIGUE: Sometimes fatigue develops because the body becomes accustomed to doing very little. People who spend significant amounts of time visiting others in the hospital will report that at the end of the day, they were exhausted though they did little to nothing during their visit. This is what happens with seasonal affective disorder, as people are repeating the same behaviors each day and their bodies are acclimating to the reduction in energy. As a result, the body's tendency is to not call for energy since it is rarely going to be used.

IRRITABILITY OR SOCIAL ISOLATION: In *The Fix Yourself Handbook*, the first book in this series, I introduced the concept of habit formation. This is your brain's way of adjusting to what you do, even if it is not a particularly good choice. There is an isolation component to seasonal affective disorder. In this case, people are environmentally isolated from each other, particularly in places where the cold weather takes over, and the brain adapts to this. Since this is a form of low-grade depression, the brain will adapt to staying away from others, and the isolation and social distance becomes a routine way of living.

FEELINGS OF WORTHLESSNESS: Again, although it is not as profound or long lived as clinical depression, seasonal effective disorder changes the way a person thinks and behaves. People with this condition do less, are unmotivated, are often not handling responsibilities, are isolating, and are simply not productive or happy. People who move from low-grade depression to seasonal affective disorder can experience exacerbated feelings of worthlessness. Suicidal attempts tend to increase during the isolation that accompanies this form of depression.

NOTE: It might be a good idea to add vitamin D3 supplements to your diet during the winter months. Check with your physician to ensure that there is no problem adding this supplement to your daily routine and to be sure that it does not interfere with any medications you may be taking.

Bipolar Disorder

There are two types of Bipolar Depression. Bipolar 1 disorder is defined by manic episodes that last for at least seven days (nearly every day for most of the day) or by manic symptoms that are so severe that the person needs immediate medical care. Usually, depressive episodes occur as well, typically lasting at least two weeks. Bipolar 2 involves at least one depressive episode lasting at least two weeks and at least one hypomanic episode lasting at least four days. Depressive symptoms include sadness or hopelessness. Hypomanic symptoms include a persistently elevated or irritable mood. The symptoms are:

MOOD SWINGS: Mood swings are the hallmark of a bipolar disorder. Previously identified as *manic depression,* it is not uncommon for the mood swings to be minor swings with some elevated emotions and intellect (Bipolar 1) to more serious swings that may last for several days. Some people with bipolar disorder report mood swings that last weeks at a time (Bipolar 2).

SADNESS: Sadness is always a part of bipolar disorder. The sadness may be mild, or it may take a person into a deep, dark place. Sometime the sadness lasts for a day; sometimes it can go on for much longer periods of time.

ELEVATED MOOD: People with bipolar disorder will experience changes in mood that may or may not have an external trigger. People may be in the throes of a depressed mood, only to find themselves becoming full of energy and energized to the point of manic episodes. These episodes may last for short periods of time or may persist for several days. Some people report manic episodes of a much longer duration.

MANIC EPISODES: Mania, unlike high energy, is something that the individual may or may not see coming and is almost impossible for them to stop. It is a kind of physical, emotional, and intellectual world on steroids. Thoughts can be disorganized, behaviors will often seem out of control, and there seems to be no regard for anyone or anything in the person's life. These may last for short periods of time, to several days, or even a week for some people.

ANGER: Anger is often a part of a bipolar disorder. As moods fluctuate and one's body teeters back and forth between depression and mania, a person may become short tempered, intolerant, and they may display angry outbursts ranging from simple verbal attacks to outright physical assaults. The intense movement back and forth between depression and the manic stages produces a tremendous strain on the body. This further exacerbates the condition.

ANXIETY: Since there is such an intense manic phase associated with bipolar disorder, anxiety will always be part of the picture. This does not have to be relegated to only the manic stage, as it is not uncommon for people with bipolar disorder to experience anxiety along with their depression.

APATHY: Where there is depression, there will be some form of apathy. However, how apathetic an individual becomes is usually related to how deeply rooted the bipolar disorder is. For people who move in and out of the mood swings quicker, the apathy can be milder. For those with more intense mood swings where the brain is experiencing considerably more trauma, apathy tends to be more pronounced.

APPREHENSION: Anytime we talk about mood swings, there will be apprehension. When one is moving back and forth between physical, intellectual, and emotional instability, they tend to worry about what will happen more often. The apprehension can be directed toward people and events in a person's life.

EUPHORIA: This is different than pure mania. Euphoria is actually a happiness that can be experienced in the manic stage, where the individual feels as though the world around them is a wonderful place to be. It is typically of short duration and tends to give way to periods of sadness and depression.

HOPELESSNESS: The movement back and forth between moods, like any situation that sets one up only to see a subsequent fall, can give way to feelings of hopelessness. This happens because even though there are periods when a person may feel elevated, have more energy, and even feel euphoric, there is always a return to the pain and sadness associated with the depressive component. As a result, it is hard to trust in the possibility of a hopeful ending. Very often, the higher a person goes, the lower is the emotional plunge that follows it.

LOSS OF INTEREST: This tends to be seen most often in the depressive part of the condition. People with bipolar disorder, especially those with Bipolar 2, will often experience an intense loss of interest. Though they are not comatose, they often appear to be one step away, with little interest in anyone or anything. In the less intense depressive episodes that we see with Bipolar 1, there is a loss of interest, but it tends to oscillate back and forth as the moods change.

IRRITABILITY: Regardless of what is occurring in a person's life when they have bipolar disorder, irritability is almost always right around the corner. The body takes a beating with this condition and as frequent mood changes place considerable energy on the body, it can produce significant increases in irritability.

RISK-TAKING BEHAVIORS: The manic stage of the disorder is characterized by rapid physical/intellectual movement, insufficient information processing, poor intellectual filtering heightened emotional states, and quick impulsive decision making. This results in behaviors that can be risky and, at times, dangerous with little regard for potential consequences.

DISORGANIZED BEHAVIOR: Unless there is an obsessive-compulsive disorder associated with the bipolar condition, people can become very disorganized as their thinking becomes fragmented and they lose interest in what is happening in their lives. There is a loss of motivation, and little things simply do not seem to matter.

AGITATION AND AGGRESSION: Bipolar disorder always includes ruminating thoughts, and those thoughts can be negative, angry, and aggressive. Oftentimes, people with bipolar disorder become agitated without any triggering device or circumstances that would typically be necessary to instigate agitated behavior. Also, since moods can turn on a dime, people react quickly, have short fuses, and can be aggressive, often without notice.

HYPERACTIVITY: In the manic stage of the disorder, people have a difficult time sitting still. Their attention quickly shifts, and they begin to engage in activities with no particular shit-off switch. They may be difficult to communicate with and may have a difficult time relaxing.

IMPULSIVITY: In the manic states, people can be impulsive since their energy level is high; they are operating at an accelerated pace and not looking at information that is coherent and well organized, or the information may be accurate, but they are misperceiving it.

They make decisions quickly and can act out seemingly without any concern for the consequences, or collateral damage.

SELF-HARM: People can harm themselves in either phase of the disorder. Depression may cause people to feel there is no way out of their pain, and they may use soothing coping devices such as cutting, burning, and other distracting self-harm behaviors to ease their emotional pain. In the manic phase, they are going so fast and can become so angry that they may inflict pain on themselves as a reaction to what is happening to them. These behaviors can become addictive and difficult for people to stop doing.

RACING THOUGHTS: Racing thoughts are very typical parts of depression. When we add the manic component, it is difficult for the brain to shut off. People report having many thoughts, often occurring at the same time, and they feel they are unable to "shut off their brains." These occur more intensely in periods of less activity, such as when they are attempting to fall asleep.

FALSE BELIEFS OR FEELINGS OF SUPERIORITY: In the manic phase, people may believe they can do just about anything. They can become arrogant, unwilling to listen to reason, and firmly believe that their position is the one that is correct. They can be condescending and, at times, abusive.

PARANOIA: With intense intellectual activity that is irrational and does not seem to have a shut-off button, people can overthink situations and begin to believe that others are against them or that horrible things are going to happen. This, as a result, may cause people to avoid being with others.

DIFFICULTY FALLING ASLEEP OR EXCESSIVE SLEEPINESS: With the transition between depressive and manic moods, it is very difficult to maintain an efficient schedule. An ever-active brain demands intense energy that is often followed by a severe drop in neurotransmitter activity, making it difficult to fall asleep on a schedule. People with this disorder will either avoid sleep, have difficulty falling asleep when they want to, will sleep too long or at times when sleeping isn't conducive to other responsibilities.

FATIGUE OR RESTLESSNESS: In another example of this back-and-forth life, one will either be so restless and unable to stop activity or be so burnt out that they are fatigued with little motivation to do much of anything. This severe fluctuation makes it difficult for family and friends to understand how the person with a bipolar condition feels because their feelings never seem to be consistent.

HYGIENE ISSUES: Depression can produce an I don't care attitude, and people in the throes of depression have a tendency to pay less attention to their personal hygiene. They may not shower for days or weeks at a time, and pay little attention to self-care rituals. They often seem disheveled, and they may have little concern with what they are wearing, or for how many days they have been doing so.

WEIGHT GAIN OR WEIGHT LOSS: Consistent with any depression-related condition, healthy eating habits do not come easy, and in this condition, a person may either overeat or not eat much at all. It is not uncommon for people with bipolar disorder to experience larger than average increases and decreases in weight depending on how intense the condition is for them.

RAPID AND FRENZIED SPEECH: In the manic phase of the disorder, people will speak in a fashion that coincides with how fast their brain is working. When that happens, their speech may seem fragmented, disoriented, rapid, and often frenzied. This may change when the manic phase ends.

SUICIDAL IDEATION: The back-and-forth movement, which is sometimes intense, is quite painful and can leave a person feeling hopeless and looking for any way out. People can become desperate, and in the impulsive and/or acutely depressive stages, they may become desperate and consider suicide as a logical solution.

Depression with symptoms of Psychosis

Major depression with psychotic features is a mental disorder in which a person has depression along with loss of touch with reality (psychosis).

DELUSIONS (DISTURBING, FALSE FIXED BELIEFS): Here, though the depression does not cause the psychosis, people who are struggling with realistic thoughts may experience periods of time when they believe something is happening or that something is true when it is not. These may range from mild to more severe, depending on the level of depression.

HALLUCINATIONS (HEARING OR SEEING THINGS OTHERS DO NOT HEAR OR SEE): In some cases, the depression may be accompanied by hearing or seeing things that are not really occurring. People may believe they see something or someone, or that someone is talking to them, or they may hear sounds or other voices. These are unseen and unheard by others.

TROUBLE THINKING CLEARLY OR CONCENTRATING: Psychosis is always accompanied by difficulty thinking and concentrating with clarity. Facts and occurrences are misrepresented, and the person's mind tends to move quickly and from item to item.

SUSPICION OR UNEASE WITH OTHERS: These symptoms can be mild with an overwhelming concern that others may be doing something to or talking about the person, or they may be more serious, as in an acute paranoia that these events are actually occurring. At times, the individual may be confrontational or aggressive in their presentation.

A DECLINE IN SELF-CARE OR PERSONAL HYGIENE: Psychosis generally carries with it a disregard for self-care and personal hygiene. People may not change their clothes, have poor bathing habits, not bathe at all, stop brushing their teeth and combing their hair, and have little to no interest in taking care of their bodies.

SPENDING A LOT MORE TIME ALONE THAN USUAL: Psychosis and social interactions are not best friends. Since the person is having trouble with reality, is suspicious and sometimes paranoid, and can be confrontational and generally unlike other people, they tend to spend more time alone and prefer it that way.

STRONG, INAPPROPRIATE EMOTIONS OR HAVING NO FEELINGS AT ALL: As mentioned earlier, a person who is psychotic will misperceive what is happening in their world, and they will formulate an internal view of that world that is not realistic. As a result, their communication and feelings are represented externally in fashions that are usually inappropriate and, at times, overwhelming. Psychotic people tend to vacillate between strong emotions and a strong willingness to express them to what seems like a complete lack of emotion. They can move from overwhelming to almost catatonic in their presentation.

PERSISTENT, UNUSUAL THOUGHTS OR BELIEFS THAT CANNOT BE SET ASIDE REGARDLESS OF WHAT OTHERS BELIEVE: A defining measure with psychotic people is that regardless of what others do to try to convince them that their thoughts are not accurate, they cannot be moved from their position. They do not trust others and firmly believe that their position is the correct one.

WITHDRAWING FROM FAMILY OR FRIENDS: Everyone can be a threat to a psychotic person. It is not uncommon for them to maintain their own space, even in the home they are living in. Those with combined psychosis and depression represent a very small part of the population. If you do feel some of the symptoms apply to you, contact your physician immediately, and make a wellness appointment.

Postpartum and Perinatal Depression

ANGER: Since hormones regulate so many of the body's systems, the imbalance that naturally occurs after childbirth can cause periods of anger that range from mild to severe and are often displayed with a quick release. Though this depression usually follows the birth of a child and can last for a year or more, some women also experience some of the same symptoms before and during their pregnancy.

ANXIETY: Many women report periods of anxiety ranging from mild to severe before and after childbirth. The anxiety is often accompanied by periods of depression.

POOR MOTIVATION: Poor motivation typically presents in any form of depression, but it can be particularly difficult for women in perinatal or postpartum depression due to the hormonal imbalance they are experiencing, along with the new demands of caring for an infant.

LOSS OF INTEREST OR PLEASURE IN ACTIVITIES: Though someone suffering from postpartum depression may have had many interests before becoming pregnant, even those may be approached with disinterest during this time.

MOOD SWINGS: Hormonal imbalance, even in the absence of pregnancy and childbirth, can cause mood swings. For some, they are mild; for others, they can be more severe. The hormonal imbalance, along with what many call the separation anxiety that results from no longer carrying a child in their womb can exacerbate an already difficult situation.

PANIC ATTACKS: For some women, the anxiety that accompanies the depression after childbirth can result in panic attacks that range from mild to severe. They may culminate during periods of extreme anxiety, but in some cases, there is no trigger and with no reasonable explanation for their onset.

FATIGUE: Some women experience an abundance of energy after childbirth. Others endure seemingly acute and chronic fatigue, which, coupled with an extended period of hormonal imbalance, can cause energy levels to remain low.

LOSS OF APPETITE: As the disinterest in so many parts of a woman's life persist, there is often a loss of appetite, and as a result, mild to severe weight loss.

RESTLESSNESS AND IRRITABILITY: Both anxiety and depression have much to do with neurotransmitter imbalance. As a woman moves back and forth between anxiety and depression, restlessness and irritability can spike. It may be a slow simmer before it happens, or it may be a very quick onset.

CRYING: Mood shifts can be mild, and they can be more severe. It is not uncommon for a woman to spontaneously begin to cry before or after childbirth as their hormones begin to fluctuate. The changes seem to come out of nowhere.

LACK OF CONCENTRATION: Consistent with any other form of depression, there is a lack of focus and concentration. This has much to do with the depressed activity in the brain. Also, there can be a lack of adequate sleep as a result of adjusting to an infant's sleep schedule.

INSOMNIA: As mentioned earlier, sleep is always a function of a schedule and the ability for the brain and the body to relax. Depression, along with the hormonal imbalance a woman is experiencing, can make it very difficult to maintain a healthy sleep schedule. Sometimes, the hormonal production will change during sleep, causing sleep interruptions. Also, since REM (deep sleep) is not being experienced efficiently, it will add to the difficulties in many aspects of a women's life during the day.

OBSESSIVE THOUGHTS: Again, the brain is not functioning efficiently, and one of the processes that neurotransmitters assist the brain in doing is a healthy expression of internal thought. This simply means that what we think about should be positive and efficient most of the time, and we should be able to stop ourselves from thinking about something. This does not always happen during periods of anxiety, depression, disrupted sleep, and hormonal imbalance.

HOPELESSNESS: Postpartum depression can be intense and unrelenting. For some women, there is a period of time where they believe that there is no way out of this and nothing they try is going to work. It can lead to periods of severe hopelessness and increased depression.

FAMILY AND SOCIAL WITHDRAWAL: There can be a general withdrawal from family and social events. In its most severe presentation, the depressed person may avoid social situation all-together, and at times, consider ending their lives.

SUICIDAL IDEATION: When hopelessness becomes a mainstay in a woman's life, thoughts of leaving become more exaggerated and leaving permanently may look like the only option left. Suicide that can become a desperate alternative for some women experiencing postpartum depression.

Time to Take Action

1. The explanation about the symptoms in this chapter are designed only to help you understand more about your depression. Don't try to act on this information yet.

2. It is easy to look at the various types of depression and find symptoms that seem to overlap. You may feel as though you have several types of depression based upon the symptom overlap. Do not try to diagnose what type of depression you have. Again, my intention here is only to help you understand the symptoms you are experiencing more efficiently. *Your particular type of depression needs to be diagnosed by a professional.*

3. Now that you are gaining a clearer understanding of the symptoms of depression, it is a good idea to follow through with that appointment with your primary care physician. Try to do that quickly.

4. Before you attend your appointment, make a list of all the symptoms you have and how you are feeling about them. The more information you give your physician, the more efficient your physician can be when it comes to helping you. Get help with this if you need it.

5. Depression is one of those conditions people want out of as fast as possible. I am presenting you with information that will help you understand your depression, and we will be moving into what to do with it shortly. If you feel that you need help immediately, call your primary care physician. If they are unavailable, get to the emergency room as fast as you can.

 **DRIVING IT HOME**

There are several types of depression, and some are more involved than others. Sometimes, your depressive symptoms may have been there for an extended period, but they were mild enough that you were able to manage them. At times, feeling the effects of depression can be the result of a triggering event and sometimes it is just a culmination of the depression wearing you down over many years. Regardless of the etiology of the condition, each type of depression can be addressed. In some cases it can be alleviated altogether. In other cases, it can be efficiently managed, and you may still live a happy and productive life. You will see this as we proceed.

YOUR DECLARATION IS: *I will begin to understand my own depression, and I will do what I need to do to conquer it!*

 **ONWARD**

We are now going to move past simple definitions of the symptoms of depression and into a more functional part of the program. In the next chapter, I am going to discuss the importance of the relationship between your body and your mind. Though we are still in the information chapters of the program, the next chapter will show you some of the things you need to do to prepare yourself for your own personal depression treatment program.

CHAPTER 4

The Body-to-Mind/Mind-to-Body Paradigm II: The Life-Changing Tag Team Duo

Understanding the power of a body and mind working together is a remarkable ally in the fight against the life thief.

PROCESSES TO EMPLOY: Brutal Honesty, I Over E, Present/Understand/Fix, Slowing Down Life's Pace, Internal Focus, Fact-Finding

IN *THE FIX YOURSELF HANDBOOK*, I DISCUSSED the importance of a healthy body. In *The Fix Your Anxiety Handbook*, I included a chapter on the body-to-mind/mind-to-body paradigm. It is an essential chapter to help you understand the importance of the reciprocal relationship between your body and your mind. Understanding this is as important for depression as it is for anxiety. In all you do, keep in mind that the relationship between your body and your mind is one of the most important relationships that keeps you in balance, healthy, productive, and happy. System balance is essential to fight depression.

I use the term body-to-mind/mind-to-body simply to illustrate the reciprocity, that back-and-forth communicative environment, that exists between your body and your mind (your brain). It is one that never stops, and understanding this shared metaphysical relationship will help you gain a clearer understanding about where your depression comes from and what you can do to help reduce and possibly alleviate it.

Put simply, your body and your mind are engaged in constant communication, and this must be so for your life to continue. This process occurs even while you are sleeping. I have made internal balance an essential theme of everything I teach. For this life-energizing process to occur, communication between the biological and psychological parts of who you are is the key factor that makes the whole circular, life-sustaining event happen. So, how does this relate to the life thief?

In Chapter 1, I introduced the notion that depression has a strong physical component associated with it and that you need to pay more attention to the physical influencers, as well as to what you are thinking and feeling. If you're following along, I provided the initial introduction to the body-to-mind/mind-to-body paradigm. Depression should always be described as a physical and intellectual/emotional condition. To do otherwise would place you at risk of not addressing one of the most important causes of this life-altering condition.

There is no real division between the mind and the body. There can never be. The reason for this is that the network of communication between the mind and the body is dynamic and never-ending. One simply cannot survive without the other. Depression exists in the framework of the communicative exercises between your body and your mind. Your depression will always be a product of your body and will also be felt by your mind.

What your body feels, and all the systems in it, are processed by your mind. So, the depressed activity that is processed in your brain will also be felt by your body. The mind-body relationship is a marvelous friendship that, at optimal levels, can provide the impetus for everything wonderful in your life. However, for this remarkable friendship to exist, it is important to learn how to create a healthy synergistic relationship between these two life-enhancing best friends. I will be addressing this in greater detail as we proceed.

Depression can reduce the efficiency of the entire human framework. As neurotransmitters are either reduced in production or produced in a state of imbalance, the signals your brain receives and subsequently sends to the rest of the body through its complex neurological pathways become compromised. The theory is that a deficiency in the neurotransmitter norepinephrine (also known as nor noradrenaline) occurs in the brain, and this deficiency may be partly responsible for creating depressed mood. More recent research suggests that there is indeed a subset of depressed people who have inadequate levels of norepinephrine. Depression is also connected to deficiencies in serotonin and dopamine.

THE TRUTH OF THE MATTER

A more complex relationship appears to exist between the three main neurotransmitters in the brain (i.e., dopamine, norepinephrine, and serotonin) and specific symptoms of *major depressive disorder*. You may note that when your physician prescribes an antidepressant, they often present it as something that will help you increase your serotonin levels. The abbreviation SSRI is meant to represent serotonin reuptake levels. Many of the antidepressants used today are designed to address serotonin issues in the brain. Some of the more sophisticated antidepressants are now being designed to target dopamine and norepinephrine as well.

All of this points to what I have been discussing, which is that depression is primarily a physical condition. This is important for two reasons:

1. It explains the origins, symptoms, and treatment modalities that may be connected to depression.
2. It dispels the myth that depression is primarily a mental disorder.

Too many people have been misled by the notion that depression is purely a mental health condition, and as the condition continues, people have a difficult time separating it from who they are. They begin to believe that their depression and who they are have become one and the same. Labeling depression as a purely mental or psychological problem could not be farther from the truth. In *The Fix Your*

Anxiety Handbook, I emphatically state that anxiety is not who you are. It is a condition that you have. Likewise, depression is not who you are. It is a condition that you have.

Some physical conditions like amyotrophic lateral sclerosis (often called Lou Gehrig's disease), Huntington's disease, and muscular dystrophy have no cures. Depression, on the other hand, has been successfully treated in thousands of people, and it can certainly be treated for you. The first step is to get away from that silly notion that there is something wrong with your brain, that this defines who you are, and that nothing can be changed. The only thing "wrong" with your brain is that it is not receiving the chemicals it needs to function at proper levels. This can be treated medicinally, and there are also many other things you can do to help break the hold of the life thief. I will be exploring this in greater detail starting in Chapter 10.

THIEVERY IN PERSPECTIVE

Depression is a physical ailment first. Remember, the reason you are depressed is a result of neurotransmitter production imbalance. In some cases, chronic pain can cause depression, and so can an improperly working thyroid gland, and hormonal imbalance. Whatever the case, the causes come from physical sources. I am by no means ruling out the impact depression has on your brain and your emotions. When you are depressed, your emotions take a huge hit, and your intellect can operate as though it is lost in space. So, there is, in fact, a huge effect on both your intellectual and emotional processes. If, however, you attempt to treat the problem emotionally or intellectually before you treat it physically reduces your chances to successfully remove the life thief from your life.

In perspective, depression starts with a neurotransmitter imbalance. This inefficient neurological stimulation affects the way your brain works. Your brain controls every system in your body, including your thoughts and emotions. When you look at all the symptoms and their explanations that I presented in Chapter 3, it is easy to see that your brain is involved in each and every one of them. They, however, have their basis in your body. You *will* experience the intellectual and emotional effects caused by the life thief intellectually and emotionally. What you are feeling there is real and should never be dismissed or undervalued in any fashion. The starting point to deal with depression, however, is with your body. This will become clear as we proceed.

 TIME TO TAKE ACTION

1. To get things started, begin to monitor what you are doing physically. Take a look at your nutrition and your sleep schedule first. Do not make any changes yet. Remember, we are still in the information stage.

2. On a piece of paper, in your journal, or on your computer, write down what you are eating each day. Also, write down what time you are getting up each day and what time you are going to bed. We are going to start simple.

3. Pay close attention to the way you speak to yourself. Internal vocalizations are motivated by internal neurological energy. If you are supplying your brain with negative energy, it has no choice but to respond in kind. Do not try to make any changes yet, but do make note of the nature of your internal dialogue.

4. If you need help with numbers one through three, enlist the assistance of someone you trust. Sometimes depression makes even the simplest of chores difficult, so don't be afraid to ask for help as you make your list and monitor your verbal expressions.

 **DRIVING IT HOME**

It is so important to understand depression as a *physical* condition. This helps you stop ruminating over where the life thief came from. It came from your body. It also stops you from fighting against yourself. There is nothing wrong with you except for the imbalance your body is experiencing. This will cause you to feel intense pressure intellectually and emotionally, but it is so important to enhance that reciprocal relationship between your body and your mind. In Chapter 12, I am going to show you how to get your physical health plans started. Doing so will not cure your depression, but it is important to remember that the healthier your body is, the better you will be able to keep the life thief from infiltrating your world.

YOUR DECLARATION IS: *It is my body and my mind. I will make both strong, and I will thrive!*

 ONWARD

As depression moves its way through your body and into your mind and emotions, it can be difficult to connect with the person you are and the world you live in. In the next chapter, I am going to examine the disconnection that occurs intellectually and emotionally as depression begins its life stealing rampage.

CHAPTER 5

Disconnected: Understanding Who's Behind the Mask, and Why

It is a harrowing experience to look into the mirror and not recognize the face staring back at you.

PROCESSES TO EMPLOY: Brutal Honesty, I Over E, Present/Understand/Fix, Slowing Down Life's Pace, Internal Focus, Fact-Finding,

---

THE SIMPLEST DEFINITION OF DISCONNECTION IS TO have one's connection with something severed. Disconnection, as I am discussing it, means to be intellectually and emotionally removed from what is happening around you in real time. Though you may experience difficulties connecting to past events and trying to make plans for what may occur in the future, the real disconnection is from what is happening around you in the present. Depression causes you to disconnect from others, and more importantly, from yourself.

People will say that they look in the mirror and either do not recognize the face staring back at them or have no real connection to it at all. That face in the mirror is emotionally blank and intellectually empty. Some of the words people have used to describe the emptiness associated with the mirror's reflection are "detached," "unresponsive," "withdrawn," and "empty." Though depression is often seen when people detach from others, from social situations, and from other external environments, the initial disconnection is realized internally first. By this, I mean that before you disconnect from your family, peers, and your external environment, you disconnect from yourself.

EMPTY REFLECTIONS

Oh my God! Someone has stolen my face! That's not me in the mirror! I can't see or feel who I am!

One of the measuring sticks of depression is the feeling of being disconnected from who you are. Most people will say that it is bad enough to feel a disconnection from others and even from society in general, but it is an entirely different matter when you feel disconnected from yourself. In all I do, I preach the notion of internal strength and that you already have all you need inside you. Depression, that life thief who wages an assault on every part of your being, gathers its own strength by disengaging you from who you are and, in the process, disconnecting you from your internal power.

By disengaging you from who you are, I mean that depression blocks your ability to connect with the unique parts of you that make you the person you are. Every person has an individualized way of thinking and feeling, and experiences varying levels of the intimate contact with the deepest part of their essence, their soul. In anatomical terms, those neurotransmitters that are not properly working are robbing your brain of its ability to perform the necessary tasks that help you connect with both your internal and external worlds. Now, reduced to a shadow of the person you used to be, you wear a mask, an internal representation to others of what you want to feel like internally, and the way you want others will see you. The mask may hide your pain, but it cannot cast out the life thief. You remain alone, a prisoner behind the mask. I will go into detail on the topic of aloneness in Chapter 7.

Emptiness is a devastating life killer. Even in times anger disappointment and vengeance you share some type of connection with what you are thinking and feeling. You may know why you are feeling these feelings, and you may even know that they are inaccurate or may hurt you or someone else. The point is you can feel them. Depression creates a world of emptiness where your mind and your feelings seem to have abandoned you and separated you from the rest of the world. Consider the following example.

Peter is a thirty-two-year old engineer. He and his former wife, Lorraine, have been separated for two years. Their marriage produced one child, Samantha, who is now eleven years old. Peter's family has a history of depression, anxiety, and suicide. During his marriage to Lorraine, Peter experienced mood swings, issues with his motivation, communication problems, procrastination, thoughts of failure, guilt, shame, and suicidal ideation. He never had a serious suicide attempt, but seriously thought about it on two occasions.

After ten years of marriage, Lorraine had enough of all the ups and downs and was concerned that Samantha would experience a home life that could lead to problems for her as her life progressed. Lorraine was beginning to see some of Peter's behaviors in her daughter. She felt that her decision to leave the marriage was in both her and Samantha's best interest. But she did leave the door open for Peter to return if he was willing to "take care of his problems."

Following a visit with his primary care physician, Peter was prescribed an introductory dose of Lexapro, which worked for several months, but the symptoms started to return. His physician increased the dosage, but the problems have persisted. Peter needs more help. He reports that he feels disconnected, out of touch with himself, and he no longer understands the person he is becoming. Nothing makes him feel good, and he cannot seem to connect with the way he feels and thinks or, for that matter, with anyone else.

Peter's case illustrates what happens when someone experiences depression to the level of intellectual and emotional disconnection. Sometimes disconnection is more subtle, with intermittent periods where the person does feel connected. However, there always seems to be a return to that flat emotionless world that seems undefined and unending. Like so many other people with depression, Peter became stuck in the shame and the guilt because of what he was doing to other people. Regardless of what he did, he could not make the depression stop. He felt alone, and misunderstood, a hopeless prisoner in the clutches of a merciless demon who would not release its hold on him.

UNMASKING THE MASK

Many people talk about the mask they wear to keep people from seeing how depressed they are and how disconnected they are from their world. There is an ironic side to depression's diversionary mask. Although it helps you put on a good face for those in your world, it makes you reliant on that good face as you live your life. Another myth about depression is that if you continue to deny those emotions that seem to be causing you pain, your brain will adjust and you can beat the life thief. Unfortunately, there is no "fake it 'til you make it" with depression. There are indeed times when you must leave the sanctity of your home, move outward, and interact with society, at which point, to some extent, you will have to put on your best face. The key, however, is not to make living your life behind the life thief's mask your long-term strategy.

No other disease or physical condition causes people to hide behind a self-manufactured intellectual and emotional deflector like the mask depression forces you to create. In almost every other disease or condition, we see people championing their fight with the condition. We see them rising up and taking arms against their vicious attacker. We watch as they exhaust every possible option to exclude the attacker from their lives and return to a healthy, happy way of living.

It almost feels like the life thief knows this and has a built-in defense system to make sure you do not become a champion with your own battle cry. This is exactly the tool it uses to break your spirit and keep you living in a world that is empty, disconnected, and full of shame and regret. In every other illness, those who are suffering are willing to wage battle. They know in their minds that they must. Without the battle, all hope is lost. The reason the life thief is so successful is because it lodges its irrational hopelessness in your brain, which, of course, is the exact organ you are using to wage war against it. So, as you attempt to attack depression on an intellectual level first, you will be doing so with a brain whose artillery—those neurotransmitters I have been talking about—has been significantly affected. In short, you have come to the battle unarmed.

So, you have a choice. You can continue to wear the mask, or you can weaponize by understanding the facts about depression, and learning how to put together a treatment plan that will help you reduce the effects brought on by the life thief. It's time to take the steps that are necessary to begin the battle. Looking back to Chapters 1 and 2, you will see many depression-related symptoms, and you can become overwhelmed by thinking that you will never alleviate all of them. Try not to take that message away from those chapters. Unless you have other predisposing physical ailments, like thyroid disease or some other hormonal imbalance, all those symptoms come directly from one source: neurotransmitter production imbalance. Any weaponry in your arsenal in the early stages of your fight against the life thief *must* target your physical concerns first.

Depression, again, is not who you are; it is a condition you have. You must attack it on a physical level first. You start this process in two ways:

1. Remove anything that works against the health of your body first. That includes all the wrong foods and schedules that do not work, poorly scheduled sleep patterns, and accelerants to try to get you going, to mention a few. Anything that can possibly energize the life thief must be removed. This should be done slowly and under the advice of a physician. Stop throwing caution to the wind and be more scheduled and more accountable when it comes to your physical health.

2. Do not just think about making an appointment with your doctor. Do it. If you are going to wage battle against a beast that has taken up residence inside your body and your mind, there is no wishy washiness allowed. If you are going to attack this, you are going to need to get serious about it.

By now, you have most likely tried many approaches, and you have taken all kinds of suggestions to banish the life thief from your world. Many of them have not worked. This time, you are not alone. I will take you through each and every step you need to take to fend off this life-stealing monster. Neither I nor anyone else, however, can do all of this for you. So, be willing to take up the sword against this unwanted adversary. Together, we can banish it from your life.

 TIME TO TAKE ACTION

1. Try not to look at the depression that has permeated your life as a hopeless state that will never end. This is going to be a step-by-step battle, and victory will not come quickly. Be willing to stay with the program I am going to teach you, and little by little, good things can happen.

2. Sometimes masks can serve a purpose. In the case of depression, they can help you do what you need to do on any given day. However, do not hide behind one. Depression is nothing that needs to be hidden from the world. If you have it, you have it. Be willing to become the champion of your own battle. We will begin to discuss our plan can help you start to build a happy and productive life in Chapter 12.

3. For now, it is important to begin arming yourself. Try to remove those items that feed the demon. Do not try to do it all at one time. Make a list of what needs to be removed from your life, and then talk about it with a friend or a family member. Get your physician involved in the process.

4. You are learning to understand that depression is primarily a physical condition. If you have not made your appointment with your physician, please do so. Be willing to do what they are suggesting. Once again, there is nothing wrong with obtaining support with this step; If necessary, ask someone you trust to attend the consultation with you.

5. Depression is a stubborn adversary. It doesn't respond to treatment quickly, and it can leave you feeling as though nothing is working. It is also hard to see any progress because *your brain is not ready to process it.* Talk about what you are doing with others. Begin the practice of communicating what you think and feel on a regular basis. Don't let the life thief occupy your brain on its own terms, and don't let it keep you alone and defenseless behind its mask.

 DRIVING IT HOME

Your life thief is an expert at disconnecting you from who you are and from the strength that resides in you. It is one of its key components; as it tears you down, it makes you feel alone in the world that seems to have become a disconnected emotional prison. Like any other physical condition, this life-stealing beast has its weaknesses. Be willing to incorporate the weapons necessary to fight the beast that is terrorizing your life, and know that you are not alone this time as you wage the battle.

YOUR DECLARATION IS: *The face in the mirror is mine. I will reclaim it!*

 ONWARD

All too often, depression leaves you feeling as though you are stuck in the mud, spinning your wheels, and going nowhere. In the next chapter, I am going to explain how being stuck physically, intellectually, emotionally, and spiritually empowers the life thief and weakens your connection with who you are. I am also going to show you how to begin looking past your own sticking point.

CHAPTER 6

Stuck in the Mud: Spinning Your Intellectual/ Emotional Wheels

Depression can leave you stuck in an impersonal dark world with nothing but feelings of shame, despair, and worthlessness.

PROCESSES TO EMPLOY: Brutal Honesty, I Over E, Present/ Understand/Fix, Slowing Down Life's Pace, Internal Focus, Fact-Finding, Forgiveness

A PERSON UNWILLING TO PARTICIPATE IN ACTIVITIES; *a curmudgeon or party pooper; one who is slow, old-fashioned, or unprogressive; an old fogey*—these are some of the typical definitions of someone who is stuck in the mud. We live a dynamic life, and it is constantly changing. Change demands transitions on our part. It necessitates moving off that safe little square, that comfort zone that keeps us protected and often in our own private world. Sometimes, being stuck in the mud means we are unwilling to move off those little squares. Unwilling does not present a truly accurate picture of what happens when a depressed person is faced with making changes in their lives. We're going to take a look at stuck in the mud on the life thief's terms in a very different way.

In this chapter, in addition to providing you with a more in depth understanding of what it means when depression has you "stuck in the mud", I also want to provide you with some information about the biology of the human brain, and what happens to your brain, and subsequently, the rest of your body, when you have depression. I will give you the basic anatomical presentation, and then I will break it down into terms you can understand. My goal is to simply help you become more knowledgeable about what's happening to you when the depression thief takes over your life. Knowing more about the anatomical processes will help you more efficiently explain what is happening you when you speak to the professionals you will be working with. It is also so important for you to use any and all information available to help you when you begin to formulate your treatment plan.

THE TORTOISE, THE HARE, AND THE LIFE

Almost everyone has heard the fable of the tortoise and the hare. In the story, the hare begins the race with the capacity to quickly shut down his opponent. After a while, however, the confident hare decides to take a nap, and the tortoise, moving in slow motion but never stopping, passes him and wins the race. If the tortoise was a person suffering from depression and the hair as the rest of the world, you would expect the rest of the world to take a nap and wait for the person with depression to catch up. But that's not what happens. There is no scenario involving the life thief where the depressed person is provided with such a gift, and wins the race. No, the depressed person *always* feels like the tortoise, struggling mightily to keep up with the rest of the world, with the weight of the world resting firmly on their back, and with the tragic feeling that they will never keep up, let alone win.

It is not uncommon for a depressed person to say that they feel like they have a ball and chain around their ankle. They are trying as hard as they can to move forward, but the scenery never changes. To understand what is happening in this stuck in the mud way of living is to understand the impact neurotransmitter imbalance has on the brain and the rest of the body. So let's get to the heart of the issue.

Let's look at the responsibilities your brain has as your life unfolds on a daily basis. In addition to being a thinking machine, the brain is also your body's central processing center. It has the responsibility of directing the activity in each and every system in your body. It is not unlike the car you drive. Regardless of whether its power it's applied by a battery or a gas run engine, energy needs to be properly supplied to your car's computer system to direct all the actions necessary to get you from one point to the other.

A healthy brain is involved in literally everything that happens in your life on any given day. It has the responsibility of guiding all eleven human organ systems: the cardiovascular system, digestive system, endocrine system, integumentary system, lymphatic system, muscular system, nervous system, reproductive system, respiratory system, skeletal system, and the urinary system. When the brain, the nervous system, and other systems are healthy, the body operates efficiently. However, let's turn our attention to what happens to your brain and nervous system when the life thief robs your brain of its ability to efficiently perform its routine daily functions.

THE MASTER THIEF AT WORK

The fuel that runs your brain and the rest of your body is significantly impacted by the level of efficiency in which the chemicals designed to stimulate your brain perform. When your brain and your nervous system are operating at full or near full capacity, there is a fully functioning reciprocal relationship between the brain and your body. Your brain sends messages to your nervous system, which runs throughout your entire body. Your brain is charged with the responsibility of helping all the systems, muscles, and other activities of the body run efficiently. To do so, it relies on efficient neurochemical production to make all of this happen.

When you are suffering from depression, the life thief, unfortunately, robs you of the chemicals—those neurotransmitters—that were meant to help your brain run all these internal relationships. Now, the fuel necessary to run your complicated neurological machine is provided at a diminished capacity. What could have been a finely tuned neurological machine has been reduced to an intellect that sputters through life, routinely skipping a beat and unable to perform even what should be the simplest of activities.

Let's take a look at the difference between a healthy neurological system and one that has been infiltrated by the life thief.

Healthy Brain and Neurological System

- Remains in relatively constant moods
- Can maintain focus and concentration
- Has good social skills
- Has good brain/body communication
- Gets things done on time
- Sustains motivation
- Connects to self and others
- Maintains good hygiene
- Can set and execute priorities
- Communicates well
- Has positive self-image and good self-esteem
- Has good short term memory
- Likes being with others
- Has good energy most of the time
- Interprets information correctly
- Makes good decisions
- Is pleasant around others
- Looks forward to tomorrow and beyond

Unhealthy Brain and Neurological System

- Has constant mood swings
- Struggles to focus and concentrate
- Has questionable social skills
- Struggles with brain to body communication
- Procrastinates
- Often lacks motivation
- Struggles to connect to self and others
- Has poor personal hygiene
- Has difficulty setting and executing priorities

- Experiences communication problems
- Has poor self-image and self esteem
- Struggles with short term memory
- Tends to isolate
- Often suffers with low energy
- Struggle to interpret information correctly
- Has a hard time making decisions
- Can be difficult to get along with
- Can experience suicidal ideation

IT'S A PHYSICAL THING

At the risk of going just a bit deep, I am going to give you the basic biology involved in all this neurotransmitter activity. Then, I will simplify the concept, but it is important to know this because it helps move you away from those myths about depression. It also gives you the factual information you need to understand what is happening to your body, and helps you understand what you need to do to move away from the notion that depression is purely a mental health problem. I am going to present some basic physiology, and then I will break it down to help you understand what's happening when you are depressed.

The Biology

Neurotransmitters are a chemical substance that are released at the end of a nerve fiber by the arrival of a nerve impulse. By spreading this impulse more widely across the synapse or junction, the neurotransmitter causes the transfer of the impulse to another nerve fiber, a muscle fiber, or some other structure. Neurotransmitters are located in the part of the neuron called the axon terminal. They are stored within thin-walled sacs called synaptic vesicles. Each vesicle can contain thousands of neurotransmitter molecules. Most of your neurons belong to the central nervous system, but some reside in the peripheral ganglia of the peripheral nervous system, and many sensory neurons are situated in sensory organs such as the retina of the eye and cochlea of the inner ear.

In Layman's Terms

Now I will translate that into a language that is a bit more understandable.

- Neurons or nerve cells are the fundamental cells of the brain and nervous system responsible for receiving sensory input from the external world, for sending motor commands to our muscles, and for transforming and relaying the electrical signals at every step in between. Neurotransmitters are chemicals that are located in a part of the neuron.

- Neurons send messages all over your body to allow you to do everything from breathing to talking, eating, walking, and thinking. They use neurotransmitters to send these messages.

- Neurotransmitters are chemical substances that are released by the neurons in response to impulses designed to help spread messages to another nerve, muscle fiber, or other physical structure in need of that stimulation.

- Most neurotransmitters reside in your central nervous system. These are the neurotransmitters that assist your brain in its normal, routine, everyday functions.

MAKING SENSE OF IT ALL

As far back as Chapter 1, I have said that depression is primary physical condition, that you are not mentally ill because you have depression, and that it should be attacked physically first before you can turn your attention to the intellectual and emotional concerns caused by the life thief. As you can see by our brief lesson in physiology, a healthy mind and body are the product of your body's healthy neurotransmitter production. When all the messages are being sent efficiently from nerve to nerve and from nerves to other body parts, we have normal mind/body functioning. However, when there is a problem with this process, the brain does not receive what it needs, and we can have *neurological depression*. Welcome to the life thief!

An essential point to remember in your fight against this happiness-stealing beast is that it thrives on your naivety. It is difficult to even make the attempt to gather information about depression or any other subject when your brain is neurologically undernourished. So, many people spin their wheels, running in circles trying to find some type of a solution to address their depression. One of the most important tools in your antidepression tool chest is knowledge. You do not need to become a medical expert, but you should begin to acquire more knowledge about what is happening to your body when depression makes its unwanted appearance. Obtaining the correct information about depression helps you take your first step in formulating the treatment plan that you are going to use to eventually change your life.

 TIME TO TAKE ACTION

1. I have been providing you with some of the accurate information you need to understand this debilitating human condition. Do not stop with what you are reading here. There are many books, scientific journals, and internet articles on the subject. Start by acquiring more information about those neurotransmitters and what is happening in your brain when you have depression.

2. Include other people in your knowledge search. Remember, you do not need to struggle alone with depression, so any help that you can enlist should always be welcome.

3. Keep notes on the information you are acquiring. You well use this information when we get the part of the program where we design a treatment plan for you.

4. Make a list of the information you find, and discuss it with your physician. Remember, the more information you bring to that setting, the better a physician can help you. Share the knowledge you are acquiring with your and, of course, all the symptoms you are experiencing.

 DRIVING IT HOME

Obtaining the correct knowledge is your first point of attack in anything you do in your life. Not knowing what to do with depression is akin to arming the life thief with all the ammunition it needs to overtake your world. It allows the thief to strike with no concern whatsoever about your ability to strike back. Obtain all the knowledge you can and share it with others. As we begin to move into the treatment part of our plan, you are going to need reinforcements. Your support network is going to be invaluable in your movement forward.

YOUR DECLARATION IS: *I will arm myself with knowledge. I will strengthen my point of attack.*

 ONWARD

What happens when your world becomes a lonely and dark place to live? What happens when there isn't a network to help you? In the next chapter, we are going to take a look at the aloneness that comes from depression, and how constructing a support network can help you in your fight against your personal life steeler.

CHAPTER 7

Leave Me Alone/Alone in the Crowd: Feeling Alone in the Darkness and What to Do About It

It is the epitome of on the outside looking in. The life-thief keeps you prisoner and isolates you from a world of happiness and joy that you cannot feel.

PROCESSES TO EMPLOY: Brutal Honesty, I Over E, Present/Understand/Fix, Slowing Down Life's Pace, Internal Focus, Fact-Finding

A TYPICAL DEFINITION OF "ALONE" IS TO be sitting by oneself, where no one else is present. It usually means that no other human being occupies the same space with us, either because no one is available or because we have chosen to remove ourselves from any other human contact. For some, having a pet nearby satisfies the need for social contact, but for most people, the concept of being alone refers to occupying a space away from other humans. In the context in which I am discussing it, "alone" has two distinctly different meanings.

1. You can be alone because you choose to be or because no one else is available, as I presented in the paragraph above.

2. You can feel alone when someone else is present or even when you are in a crowd.

It is the second type of aloneness that we will discuss in this chapter. In Chapter 6, I discussed how the life thief makes its devilish appearance as a result of neurotransmitter problems and how it affects the way the brain, nervous system, and other body components operate. Under the symptom list in Chapter 2, I defined an important symptom that comes from this chemical imbalance: your inability to connect with yourself and feel part of others and the world you live in. I am describing aloneness as *being intellectually, emotionally, and spiritually disconnected from oneself and the outside world.*

One of the most important themes in *The Fix Yourself Handbook* is the concept of internal balance. Internal balance occurs when our physical, intellectual, emotional, and spiritual attributes can operate in equilibrium. In that book, I mentioned that another concept of internal balance can be found in Buddhist texts described as a feeling of nirvana. Regardless of what terminology you choose to use, any system's balance relies on the neurotransmitters that stimulate the brain, the nervous system, and the rest of the body to operate efficiently.

A debilitating symptom that occurs when this does not happen is the disconnectedness I discussed earlier. In more severe cases, it can evolve into a state of aloneness. People with depression will speak of being alone in a crowd, or being on the outside looking in. Others will make jokes and laugh almost uncontrollably, but the depressed person is not moved by the humor. The social world is merely spinning around them, and they feel out of step, not really part of the merriment. Depression's kind of aloneness does not require a separation from other humans: the aloneness felt by those affected by the life thief can cause them to feel withdrawn and friendless in even the most loving intimate and social situations. They can feel as though they are simply not there.

THE CONNECTION TWO-STEP

Very often, people who are suffering from depression-related aloneness attempt to solve the problem by allowing themselves to be pulled into social situations. This usually occurs because their family and friends realize that the person is spending too much time alone and want to help them connect with other people. Sometimes this eases the symptom just a bit, but for the most part, even if there is some relief, it is short lived, and the depressed person returns to the thief's world and their aloneness.

One of the reasons trying to be social with others first does not work is because doing so skips the first step of the connection process. The first step in connecting with the external world and those who occupy it is to connect with yourself. The reason others seem so happy in social situations is that, on some level, they are connected with their internal self. This does not mean that they are comfortable with themselves: it only means that they don't suffer from the reduction in neurotransmitter activity and, as a result, they can think and feel on a level that helps them to connect internally. They do not feel the internal disconnect brought on by depression.

This does not mean that being social with other people is not a good thing if you have not connected with yourself yet. Any social activity or time spent with other people can help. At the very least, it temporally removes you from the darkness of the thief's pitch black world. Any reprieve, even short ones, is a blessing. However, you are looking for something with a bit more shelf life, something that can help turn on the lights in the life thief's torture chamber. The first step is to do the work to connect with yourself. This brings us back to that physical component that has to be corrected.

TAKING THE FIRST STEP

Since the disconnection and loneliness come directly from the lack of neurotransmitter stimulation in the brain, the first step is obviously to start there. Sometimes your genetics could be at the heart of the problem. Other times, something may have gone wrong with your thyroid gland or anything that can affect the hormone levels in your body. Let's look at an example.

Helen is a single twenty-eight-year-old woman who lives alone and has a managerial position in an advertising agency. She is prone to bouts of low-grade depression, but always seems to be able to work her way through it. For about five days every month, she goes into a significantly deeper depressed mood. Her motivation is down, she gets angry easier, she is ruminating more, and she is not always a very pleasant person to be around. Helen's increase in depressive symptoms is the result of her menstrual cycle. Many women can experience this. The main culprit is a change in hormone production that, for some people, can instigate an increase in their depressive symptoms.

In Helen's case, the increase in her depression can be traced directly to a hormonal imbalance that occurs monthly for short periods of time. For Helen to address the increase in her depressive symptoms, she needs to address the hormonal imbalance. It would make sense for her to visit her gynecologist and have a blood analysis done to determine the course of action. It might be a light antidepressant or a birth control pill, and her gynecologist might advise some dietary changes. Notice that all of these are *physical* remedies to Helen's monthly increase in depressive symptoms.

On a grander scale, if you are suffering from depression in which the symptoms are more intense and longer lasting, your need for a comprehensive physical workup is essential. It is important to know if anything is affecting you physically, and if your depression is caused or exacerbated by something other than neurotransmitter imbalance. It is also important to identify people who are experts in the field of depression to help you with the diagnosis. These people will know what tests to conduct and how to interpret them. For example, if you visit an endocrinologist to have your thyroid checked your numbers may lie *within normal ranges*. It is important to ask exactly what those numbers are, since thyroid numbers on the lower end of the normal range can be suggestive of an increase in depression symptoms.

Let's take a look at the steps you should take to determine if physical problems are either causing or making your depression feel worse.

ATTACKING THE BEAST 101

A visit with your physician is crucial. However, you should not only be looking for something that may cause depression. You want a full body workup with all the relevant blood tests performed, even those that do not directly pertain to depression. Sometimes a doctor will focus on the cause of your depression, which may keep them from focusing on physical problems that are not directly related to depression but may be involved with its presentation.

It is wise to incorporate specialists in your diagnostic plan. These might include a psychologist who specializes in depression: an endocrinologist to examine your thyroid: a gynecologist or someone who specializes in hormones: a specialist who understands gut health, since much of what goes on in the body is related to what occurs in the gut: and a sleep specialist to determine if you are both getting enough sleep and if, during your sleep cycle, you are getting enough REM sleep. Even if these people do not give you all the answers you are looking for, it is so important to rule out whatever is not part of the problem.

Let's look at the list of necessary procedures to begin determining how your own physiology either causes or effects your depression. Before you move deeper into the program and begin to discuss your treatment the plan, you will need to take these steps.

THE FOUR STEPS TO START YOUR DEPRESSION TREATMENT PLAN

1. Remember, you are the patient, and the professionals you are visiting work for you. It is one thing to make appointments with these professionals, but you must hold them accountable and make sure they are giving you the level of treatment you deserve. Depression often interferes with your ability to be tenacious enough to hold others accountable, so do not be afraid to enlist the services of people who can represent your concerns efficiently to these professionals. These professionals need to be thorough, and they need to be willing to spend as much time with you as is necessary.

2. As I advised in Chapter 7's action steps, make a list of every symptom or concern that you have. Share and discuss that list with your advocate, that person who is going to be attending appointments with you. This person, at times, can be a friend, or a family member, but there are cautions when it comes to family members. I will discuss more about your advocate in Chapter 10. Make sure that every item on that list is explained to the physician and that they give you an in-depth explanation of why that symptom or concern exists. If they cannot, they need to prescribe the testing or provide referrals to other professionals to clarify that concern. You have symptoms and concerns, and you need answers.

3. It is vital that you take someone with you to your appointments. Depression will make it easy for a professional to talk over you. They may assume that you have a mental health concern and that and that you are not clearly presenting your symptoms, or that you may be exaggerating or grasping at straws. Make sure the person going with you understands what you are feeling and that day can represent that position in no uncertain terms to the professional you are seeing.

4. If you have concerns about how you are being treated by a professional, do not be afraid to seek a second opinion. This is your life, you are important, and you have the right to the best care that can possibly be available for you. Let no one tell you otherwise.

Depression can be a dark and ugly place from which to live your life. The life thief relishes keeping you in the dark world it has created for you. Becoming knowledgeable about your condition is the first step, as we have discussed in the previous chapters. Learning how to take that information and presenting it to the professionals who can help you diagnose existing and potential problems is an important next step in putting the chains on this life thief. It seems like a big step, but remember, you are no longer alone.

You are in pain, you need answers, and you are going to get them. That is the mindset you need to maintain. Enlist the help of someone you trust to help you present your case to the professionals who are helping you. Never let anyone invalidate what you are telling them or provide you with anything less than the best care.

TIME TO TAKE ACTION

1. Understand the difference between being alone and aloneness as it relates to depression. If you are having difficulty connecting to yourself, if you feel alone and unconnected to others, ask someone you trust to help you make the appointments with the necessary professionals.

2. Approach your visit with each professional with the understanding that you must provide all the information necessary for you to understand your problem, and you must be willing to represent yourself with the expectation of quality professional care. Make them give you their undivided attention, empathy, and commitment to help you work toward solutions.

3. Schedule all the various appointments for a full-body workup. These visits may include your primary care physician, endocrinologist, gynecologist, psychologist, sleep specialist, and anyone else who can help you determine what physical factors may be related to your depression. You may need help with this, so do enlist someone you trust to advocate for you. Start with your visits with your primary care physician. If you are having trouble with this person, make an appointment with someone new. Your insurance company may determine that these tests need to be provided one at a time. Do not be discouraged. The point is to get all of them done.

4. Remember that these health care professionals work for you. Hold them accountable for obtaining and providing you with the best care based on accurate information. They may or may

not give you answers immediately, but do make sure that the physician or other professional cover all the bases when it comes to your care.

5. Do not be afraid to schedule visits with other professionals for second opinions, if necessary.

 DRIVING IT HOME

No one needs to stay alone and in the clutches of the life thief. Even if you think you have tried everything you can to address your depression, if it is still there, then it requires more care. Try not to find yourself stretched to the end of your rope and deciding that there is no way out of the darkness. There is a solution, and if you are still suffering from depression, you simply have not found yours yet. Remove yourself from the loneliness of the depression by inviting others in to help you. Never, even for a moment, feel as though you are not worth it, because you are.

YOUR DECLARATION IS: *I am going to get the answers I need, and nothing is going to stop me!*

 ONWARD

As you are doing what you need to do to diagnose your depression and beginning to take the steps to formulate a treatment plan, it is important to understand the relationship between depression and anxiety. For some, it can feel like facing a tag-team duo; as one takes you up, the other takes you down. For others, the symptoms are less pronounced. In the next chapter, I will provide you with the information you need to understand the relationship between anxiety and depression and how that relationship can affect you.

CHAPTER 8

Cousins in Crime: The Depression/Anxiety Relationship

It's a tag-team relationship that has you bouncing back and forth, going up and down in a relentless world that plays with your emotions, and recks your brain.

PROCESSES TO EMPLOY: Brutal Honesty, I Over E, Present/Understand/Fix, Slowing Down Life's Pace, Internal Focus, Fact-Finding, Patience

DEPRESSION AND ANXIETY, THOUGH THEY SEEM TO be oppositional conditions, have a reciprocal relationship, and it is rare to find one present without the other. Sometimes depression leads to anxiety, and sometimes it is the anxiety that burns you out and leads to depression. Sometimes they have a concurrent onset. By reciprocal relationship I mean that they can either occur together, or that one instigates another, and also that they may be present in your body at the same time, but that one is the dominating condition. The other can either be a result of the first condition, but it can still exert some type of influence over what you are thinking and feeling.

One of the reasons depression can be difficult to diagnose is due to the interplay between depression and anxiety. Throughout this book thus far, I have discussed neurotransmitter imbalance, and up to this point, I have applied it directly to your depression. However, it is important to keep in mind that, as I stated as far back as Chapter 1, the chemicals that stimulate your brain enable it to run *every* system in your body. Since your brain is involved in everything you do, it stands to reason that it will also be involved in the way you feel, and anxiety comes under that heading, even when your primary condition is depression.

KINGPIN, TAG TEAM, OR FALL OUT

When your brain experiences a deficit of the transmitters it needs to run properly, it becomes susceptible to a wide variety of conditions. Since your brain runs virtually everything the body does, when it is not running at optimal levels, every system in your body can suffer. Imbalanced neurotransmitter production opens the door for depressed neurological activity, which can cause the brain to move back and forth between depression and anxiety. Which position either occupies depends on the dynamics of your own personal life thief.

Neurotransmitter imbalance leaves the brain in a vulnerable position. When it does not receive the chemicals it needs, it becomes more susceptible to invasions, both internal and external. Now, with depressed activity in the brain, its defenses against depression and anxiety are significantly reduced, and each can play a more pronounced rule in your life. Neurotransmitters like serotonin, norepinephrine, and dopamine not only help balance the brain and give it the ability to perform its daily functions efficiently, but they also act as a defense system against assaults on the brain, particularly those related to depression and anxiety. With the brain's defenses reduced, either or both can make their dastardly appearances and wreak havoc in your otherwise healthy neurological ecosystem.

The Kingpin

With defenses down and neurological activity depressed, the brain is an easy target for depression in some form. For the purposes of our discussion, let's make depression our kingpin—that is, the dominant attacker. When the chemicals that contribute to your brain's balance, and likewise, its feeling of peace and tranquility, are compromised, system-wide depression can take over your world. The brain simply does not have enough strength to fight it off. You begin to experience the symptoms that correlate to your own personal life thief. Refer back to Chapters 1 and 2 to refresh yourself on the types of depression and their symptoms.

The interesting, and often untold story about the depression is that it can so drastically devastate the body that it leaves it open to other attacks. Some of those attacks include other physical ailments like joint and muscle pain, gastrointestinal issues, and migraines, to name a few. The carnage depression wreaks on your mind and your body, also opens the door for the anxiety demon to rear its ugly head. Now, instead of one debilitating attacker, you may be experiencing two.

In *The Fix Your Anxiety Handbook*, I list the primary symptoms of anxiety. Without going into a long explanation of those symptoms, this is what you can expect.

The Symptoms of Anxiety

- Excessive worrying
- Restlessness and difficulty sleeping
- Concentration issues tension
- Irritability and tension
- Fatigue
- Increased heart rate and palpitations
- Sweating and hot flashes
- Trembling and shaking
- Chest pains and shortness of breath
- Feelings of terror or impending doom

For those who experience bipolar depression, much of this makes sense. In cases of Bipolar 1, you may move back and forth between periods of depression and periods of increased energy in which you experience mild anxiety symptoms. For those suffering from Bipolar 2, the depression-anxiety tag team is far more aggressive. The key takeaway from this section is that in almost every form of depression, there can be at least a touch of anxiety. Sometimes the anxiety makes you feel as though you do not have depression, since it instigates mild reprieves that are built into the depressive episodes.

Sometimes, anxiety presents as increased worry, obsessive thoughts, difficulty turning off your brain, and a bit of physical acceleration, though typically short lasting. For some people, however, after depression takes its toll, they are thoroughly beat up. They may find themselves overwhelmed by some of the anxiety symptoms. Some people will experience rapid mood changes and may find themselves crying for no apparent reason. Sometimes it is just the depression that causes the mood swing. Other times, it is the fluctuation back and forth between depression and anxiety that causes the swing.

The Tag Team

For some people, depression and anxiety present at the same time, and with almost equal force. This does not only apply to Bipolar 2 cases. Those suffering from Bipolar 2 will often report reasonably constant stretches of depression followed by a reasonably long period of mania. When anxiety and depression present together, people will report having the symptoms of both anxiety and depression occurring at the same time. For example, you might present with the depressive symptoms like difficulty concentrating, fatigue, poor appetite, procrastination, thoughts of shame and guilt, feelings of terror or impending doom, restlessness and difficulty sleeping, and suicidal ideation.

You may note that some of these symptoms appear on both lists. I have chosen just a few of them to illustrate the crossover. The interesting component of the tag-team phenomenon is that not only are you experiencing symptoms of both anxiety and depression, but the crossover in symptomology makes it more difficult to diagnose your depression. People often say they are not sure they have depression because they assume depression presents with symptoms of sadness, disconnection, isolation, darkness, and feeling stuck.

So, when the symptom crossover occurs, it is not uncommon to be unsure of what is affecting your life. Bear in mind that while the crossover in symptoms is occurring, they can very naturally blend together, leaving you unaware as to which is the dominant symptom. The best way to identify the kingpin—that dominant disorder—is to just simply think about which condition is there most often and which one has a more dominant effect on your life most of the time.

Usually when anxiety is the primary diagnosis, you can feel depression following the burnout from the anxiety's intensity. On the other hand, depression makes way for anxiety-based symptoms simply because the brain is open to them. The neurotransmitter reduction causes your brain to operate at seriously reduced efficiency and as a result, the potential for anxious symptoms increases.

The Fallout

When depression takes over your world, your brain cannot use its powers to its maximum potential. This means, as I have noted previously, that every system in the body is operating at levels that are not conducive to healthy functioning. An important point when this happens is that even though you are depressed, and you are not using your intellectual faculties efficiently, you are aware that you are depressed and that something is very wrong.

You may not understand everything that is going on in your world. You may not know what to do about it, but you are very definitely aware that you are in pain and that your world is not operating properly. You may be experiencing many of the symptoms of depression, some of them to their extremes, and you may become exhausted and hopeless. This brings on a kind of surrender that can invite other conditions to more efficiently invade your life. It is as though your brain simply does not work anymore. It just doesn't seem to care. This is where anxiety comes in. Your brain is not receiving the neurotransmitters it needs, and its activity has become depressed—that is, not working at optimal levels. Your defenses are down, and here comes anxiety. You can also become anxious because it's a persistent condition that does not seem to stop, you don't know what to do about it, and there seems to be no logical way out of it. You want to run away from it, but you can't.

As if it weren't enough that depression has taken over your world. Now, you are being faced with the possibility that anxiety, on some level, is also part of the invasion of your brain. It is very easy to become overwhelmed by the possibility of two neurological demons infesting your brain. Let me offer something that puts it all in perspective: I have emphasized neurotransmitter imbalance as a physical condition. This is exactly where you need to keep your attention. Regardless of whether depression, anxiety, or both are affecting your life, everything comes from one specific physical problem: you have a neurotransmitter imbalance. **Focus your attention right there.** Addressing that will address both demons. I will show you how to do this as we progress in the program.

In Chapter 3, I emphasized that at this point in the process, you are merely gathering information that is going to help you formulate your treatment plan. That anxiety may be part of your depression is not something to be overly concerned with now: it is simply another one of the facts you will need to be dealing with to properly slay the life thief. Remember, we are gathering knowledge we will use for your treatment plan. Again, try to leave it right there for now.

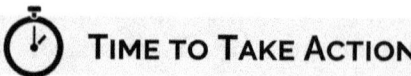 **TIME TO TAKE ACTION**

1. Anxiety and depression are different and seemingly oppositional conditions, but they can coexist. Identifying whether one or both is occurring in your life is the first step in formulating an efficient treatment plan to address them. Try to put this information where you put everything else I have been giving you: in the newly activated knowledge section of your depression database.

2. There are two ways to approach the information I am presenting about anxiety and depression occurring together. You can say, "Great, now I have another condition," or you can say, "Great, now I have more information to move forward." Focus on the second one.

3. Make a list of your symptoms again. Now, include any that seem to be related to anxiety. Try not to obsess about them.

4. Discuss your symptoms with the people close to you. When you do attend those consultations with the physicians as we discussed in the last chapter, this adds more information to your information arsenal. They will need as much as you can provide.

 DRIVING IT HOME

As we move deeper into our discussion about depression, you may be introduced to information you never heard before. Some of it may lead you one of those "ah ha!" moments, while some may leave you feeling intimidated. The very fact that you have depression can make information seem intimidating and overwhelming. This is why you want to build a network of people who can help you. For now, we are only putting together the information. Very soon, I am going to start making it a little more personal for you.

YOUR DECLARATION IS: *The right information will make me understand who I am, and I will have what I need to fight the life thief!*

 **ONWARD**

I have discussed considerable information related to depression, some in general terms, and some more specifically. It is time to take a look at your own personal life thief. In the next chapter, I will make things a little more personal as I start to prepare you for your depression treatment plan.

CHAPTER 9

My Personal Nemesis: Darkness with an Individual Touch

Get to know your own personal life thief. It's the first step in bringing light into depression's dark world.

PROCESSES TO EMPLOY: Brutal Honesty, I Over E, Present/Understand/Fix, Slowing Down Life's Pace, Internal Focus, Fact-Finding, Truth-Telling, Comfortable With Being Uncomfortable, Trust

BY NOW, YOU HAVE PROBABLY HEARD THE STATEMENT that you are a creation unique unto yourself. There is only one of you genetically: therefore, no one will experience anything in the world the same way you do. Even in the case of identical twins who share the same DNA, there will be slight differences physically, and in the way they experience the world. Your personal combination of genetics and environment makes you that unique creation, different from anyone else in the world.

In Chapter 1, I noted that there are generalized symptoms attached to depression. This means that, for the most part, everyone will experience them. If you have depression, you may feel stuck, have difficulty focusing, experience mood swings, etc. Most symptoms of depression are symptoms everyone can experience in one way or another. You, however, are going to experience the effects of depression based on your own personal life thief, and how you, yourself, interpret and experience it.

It is that combination of your own personal genetics and what you experience in your life that will create your own personal depression. This will be depression that is specific solely to you. No one else will experience it the way you do. There will be similarities regarding what and how you and others experience depression but no one else has your DNA, the circumstances of your life and theirs are not exactly the same, and the way you experience your life events will be different.

Generalized depression symptoms are those symptoms that, for the most part, everyone with depression experiences. Refer back to Chapter 2 if you feel you need to refresh yourself. Personalized depression symptoms apply specifically to you. Since depression is primarily a physical condition. No two people have exactly the same body, and no two people process their depression the same way physically.

Likewise, no two people think exactly the same way, process on an emotional basis exactly the same way, or have the same experiences. Your depression then is unique to your body, your mind, your emotions, and the way you process on a spiritual level. For depression and its symptoms to qualify as personalized, they should meet the following criteria:

1. They are a product of your own personal DNA.

2. They are interpreted by your own personal intellectual database.

3. They are subject to the way your emotions are personally expressed.

4. They are influenced by the way you process spiritually.

5. They are influenced by the way you relate to the people in your life.

6. They are influenced by the events you have experienced in your life.

Personalization by the Numbers

To help you gain a more in-depth understanding of depression's personalization criteria, I will explain each of them in greater detail.

1. They are a product of your own personal DNA.

Deoxyribonucleic acid (DNA) is the molecule that carries genetic information for the development and functioning of an organism. Your genes, or genetic markers, are part of your DNA. Though two or more human beings may be products of the same parents, their genetic markers will not be the same. This may not always apply to identical twins, but it still makes sense to treat them and their depression personally. The main takeaway is that, genetically, we are all different. This will influence how your own personal depression is experienced, since physically, your genetic makeup has a unique impact on the way your body works and how you live your life.

2. They are interpreted by your own personal intellectual database.

We all perceive the people and events in our lives differently. Our own genetics contribute to this, while the individual perspective from which we experience people and events in our lives contributes to the rest. The human mind is capable of complex modes of thought and applies that thought to almost everything we do. For some of us, we can be nonchalant about certain people and events, while others will apply significantly more thought to the level and experiences. Two people can witness the same event and have very different perceptions, and subsequently they will provide different reports about what they experienced. In short, each person's mind operates differently, so depression will be perceived and interpreted differently by different people.

3. They are subject to the way your emotions are personally expressed.

Emotions refer to the way you feel about something. They are closely attached to your reactions to what you experience in your environment. You also have a particular way you feel about yourself. You internalize feelings about whatever occurs in your life, and depression, as potent as it can be, is something you will have your own personal feelings about. You will feel it differently from other people because you feel everything else differently. No two people feel what is happening in their life, internally and externally, in exactly the same way. They will not feel their depression the same way, either.

4. They are influenced by the way you process spiritually.

When I refer to spirituality, I am talking about the connection to your essence, that core of your existence. Some people champion it, while others deny it altogether. However, your approach to it is an extremely personal experience. How much the spiritual part of our nature influences depression is unknown, but since it is one of the major facets of your human experience, it will have an impact on depression, and that impact that will be unique to you.

5. They are influenced by the way you relate to the people in your life.

Unless you are a recluse and never see anyone, other people will have an impact on the way you think, feel, and behave. You will have relationships that may be different from other people's, and you will experience and interpret those relationships differently. Some of them may be positive, while others may have a negative impact on your life. Regardless of the nature of your interaction with others, you will experience and interpret them differently than other people. Whereas genetics influence you internally, the people you interact with will have an external effect on the way your life progresses and subsequently on the way you perceive, interpret, and live with your depression.

6. That they are influenced by the events you have experienced in your life.

I always say that life is a dynamic and ever-changing enterprise. As life continues to happen around you, you will experience events that help shape your life and the way you live it. What you experience externally does have an impact on your intellect and our emotions, and both internal and external experiences will have an impact on how your depression presents, the way you experience it, and the way you think and feel about it.

IT BEGINS

Often, when people try to explain how their depression feels to other people, they always seem to come up short. Now, you can understand why this occurs. Although there are symptoms that may be classified as general and can be felt by everyone with depression, no one experiences them in the same way. You are indeed a unique entity onto yourself. No one in the world is like you, and no one will experience depression like you. Your depression is yours and yours alone. Attempting to treat your depression via an overused, one-dimensional approach that is misapplied universally to everyone yields tenuous results, at best. If are going to be serious about reducing the life thief's influence in your life, then it is time to get personal.

In recent years, the medical field began employing genetic testing to determine which medications would be most efficient in treating conditions like depression and anxiety on an individualized basis. The results of the tests produce a list of medication that can either be efficacious, marginally successful, ineffective, or could be toxic for the person being tested. So, even at the physical level, we are seeing the beginnings of a more personalized approach in the clinical treatment of depression.

Now it is time to arm yourself with the information that can accurately represent you as a unique individual and your depression as a unique product of that individuality. To treat you as nothing but a generalized case, and to attempt to treat your depression in cookie-cutter fashion will almost always fail. You are not a clone, and you experience depression differently from anyone else on the planet. Look at your depression as your personal depression and formulate a treatment plan that addresses what you are thinking and feeling with an individual approach designed just for you. Yes, it is more involved than treating it with the old, stereotyped treatment approaches, but you are worth all the effort it takes.

TIME TO TAKE ACTION

1. No one on earth is exactly the same as you are. Your depression then is not the same as anyone else's. As you move forward, keep that point in mind: quick-fix, generalized approaches will not work. Start focusing your efforts on who you are personally. Tell them how depression is affecting you physically, emotionally, intellectually, and even spiritually. Be specific if you can. You may need some help. Do not be afraid to use your network. Don't be discouraged if this is difficult for you in the beginning. Just get the process started.

2. Get your network involved now. It is important for them to understand the new personalized approach, how it applies to you, and what they can do to help you as you move forward.

3. At this point, if you have not done so, schedule that consultation with a psychologist or a counselor who specializes in the treatment of depression. This person who can help you identify those unique parts of yourself that need to be included in your treatment plan. If you already have a counselor, discuss what I am presenting here with that person.

 **DRIVING IT HOME**

You have depression, so you have a personal life thief, one that is a product of the person you are. By defining those key points I mentioned earlier in this chapter, you will begin to define the information you need to start building a personal treatment plan for your depression. That personal treatment plan will be the product of the individual way you perceive your life physically, intellectually, emotionally, and spiritually. Each and every one of those points is important, and each and every one of them can help you define who you are. It is time to get personal and to begin to formulate the plan to send this life thief packing.

YOUR DECLARATION IS: *"I will define who I am, I will build my treatment program for me, and I will rid my world of the life thief."*

 **ONWARD**

Now that you have the personal foundational information you need, it is decision time. Depression has left you beat up, often directionless, and unsure of what to do next. As we compile all the information you need to rid yourself of this menacing life thief, it is time to make a decision to stay committed, refuse to give up, and get healthy. In the next chapter, we are going to talk about how to make that happen.

CHAPTER 10

Not Giving In: Making the Decision to Get Healthy

It all starts with a decision. Decide that nothing is going to stop you and that you are going to rise above the pain that has defined you.

PROCESSES TO EMPLOY: Brutal Honesty, I Over E, Present/Understand/Fix, Slowing Down Life's Pace, Internal Focus, Fact-Finding, Risk-Taking, Commitment, Eliminating Toxic People, Life's Natural Flow, Incremental Forward Movement

---

EVERY GREAT INVENTION AND EVERY GREAT ACCOMPLISHMENT all came down to one person's decision to do something. If you are going to accomplish it, you first need to decide to do so. All too often, we have a good idea of what we want, but we never take the time to research what needs to be done to make that happen, and we go into our endeavors haphazardly and with no viable plan to arrive at our goal. If you suffer from depression, that may be what happened as you attempted to remove the life thief from your world. Without adequate information and a viable plan to follow, failure was inevitable.

I have dedicated the first nine chapters of this book to help you understand the information you need to address your depression. You now know that there are several types of depression, and each of them have symptoms, some of which are specific to one type of depression and some that overlap with other types. You have a better understanding of the mind-to-body connection, you know you must treat depression as a physical problem first, you are familiar with the relationship between anxiety and depression, and you now know you must get personal as you attack the depression monster.

Up to now, you have been spinning your wheels, going aimlessly in circles as you desperately tried to do anything you could to make your depression go away. You needed more information to understand yourself better, establish a direction, and formulate a plan to become healthy and free yourself from the chains that depression has wrapped around you. You have much of that information now, and you also know that you need a network of support people and professionals to help you formulate and implement your personal treatment plan.

The next step is yours. Depression makes it easy to do next to nothing. Your motivation is dwindling, it has been hard to gather and understand the information you need to move forward, and you were trying to do so much of this alone. Sometimes being alone meant there was no one to help you, and sometimes it meant that you were not communicating enough information to help others understand what was happening. It created an aloneness that, at times, was horrifying. So now, it is time to decide to use that information to create and use a network of people to help you through this. It's time to free yourself from snare set by your personal life thief.

INCREMENTAL: ONE STEP AT A TIME

In everything I teach, I preach the notion of incremental forward movement—that is, progressing one step at a time to eventually arrive at a goal. All too often, people struggle with formulating and implementing their plans because they are obsessed with the goal, not with the steps it takes to get there. It is very easy to become overwhelmed with the information you are receiving. One of the most important points about moving forward with your treatment plan is to understand how to implement it *one step at a time*.

You are not going to do this alone. So, the first step in the process is to decide that you will become healthy, that you are going to remain committed to the program, and that you are not going to quit. Up to now, you knew with all your heart that you wanted the depression to stop. You could not decide how to do so because there was not enough information available to you, and you had no one in your corner to help you. That changes now. Your decision to move forward must carry with it your understanding that this will not be a quick-fix program, that it will take some time to implement, but that it can help you keep depression at bay for the rest of your life.

Depression is not something that suddenly entered your life. Either you were born with it, you had a triggering event that set it in motion, or it was something that was simmering in you for some time and gradually worsened. Depression will not leave your life on its own, and you will not rid yourself of this menacing condition quickly. However, the decision to fight the beast and to stay committed to doing so is an important first step in the battle against this relentless, life-sucking foe.

BUILDING YOUR SUPPORT NETWORK: STEP 1

Making the decision to do the work to banish the life thief now calls for your first step in setting up your support network—those professionals, family members, and friends who you are going to involve in your treatment plan. This treatment plan is the exact strategy you will follow unwaveringly to create the healthy life you have always wanted. I first broached this subject in the action steps in Chapter 9. There, I mentioned choosing that one trusted person who will help you set up the rest of the network.

This person will help you identify those professionals you need to include in your program, help you schedule appointment with those professionals, and, if necessary, attend the initial consultations with them. This person should be one you can count on to be there for you. Call this person your *personal advocate*. This person should be someone who, based on your communication with them, has a reasonable understanding of what you are thinking and how you are feeling. It should not be someone you are emotionally attached to, such as family members you have a difficult history with. They do not have to understand the entire picture; that is what the professionals are for. *The function of your advocate is to understand what you are saying and to help you select and communicate with your network of treatment professionals.*

These are the three steps the advocate will help you with. I will be providing you with a detailed explanation of your support network in Chapter 15.

1. Make a list of each and every symptom you are having. Show your advocate the list in Chapters 1 and 2 to help them understand what you are experiencing.

2. Based on the symptoms you and your advocate identify, begin a list of those professionals who can help. Your list should be generalized, initially. By that, I mean you do not need to identify the exact professionals who will be providing services; you only need to identify what kind of professionals need to be involved at this point. You should start with your primary care physician. They will conduct your initial evaluation, and they can also help you identify potential members of your professional network. Your advocate should attend the appointments with your primary care physician.

3. Help you explain to your primary care physician, and eventually other professionals, what you are thinking and feeling, and as much additional information as you can provide them with.

Based on your symptoms, your list of professionals might include: *

➤ A primary care physician

➤ A psychologist or professional counselor

➤ A psychiatrist if medicines might be part of your treatment plan

➤ An endocrinologist for the possibility of thyroid issues

➤ A gastrointestinal specialist to ensure that your gut is healthy

- A hormone specialist to determine if your hormones are being produced properly
- A gynecologist to help address issues related to menstrual cycles and female hormones
- An alternative medicine professional, should you choose to include alternative medicines in your program

*Not all of these professionals may be necessary, but it's advantageous to identify them in case you need them.

THE PROFESSIONAL NETWORK

Very often, people suffering from depression begin to feel relief when they include both a physician and psychologist or professional counselor who understand the dynamics of the condition in their network. Incorporating both allows you to first identify the physical problems that need to be addressed, and incorporates a counseling component so you can begin to discuss your symptoms and how they apply to you personally. A professional counselor will also provide you with coping mechanisms and strategies to ease you through the earlier stages of your counseling program.

If you are still dealing with severe depression symptoms despite having consulted a primary care physician and a counselor, it makes sense to start including others in your plan. This will become clear as we proceed.

As I mentioned earlier, your primary care physician should prescribe a blood analysis to determine if any physical problems may be causing or contributing to your depression. They may prescribe an antidepressant to get you started. If antidepressants are going to be part of the picture, it makes sense to undergo genetic testing to determine what medicines to apply initially. Genetic testing is not perfect, but it is better to have an idea of what drugs best suit your personal genetic make-up, rather than to make it a hit-or-miss proposition.

If you are not sure about the rest of your list of professionals, very often, your primary care physician can make suggestions or give you referrals. Ask your advocate to help your primary care physician ensure that other professionals receive any information such as blood tests, etc. Good communication among professionals goes a long way to helping you solve your depression issues. Make sure you and your advocate have a good rapport with your primary care physician, as this is the individual who will be at the center of your treatment plan.

Depression cannot be diagnosed in under ten minutes. Today's medical model, particularly when doctors are employed by hospitals, stresses getting people in and out quickly. Keep in mind, once again, that your practitioners work for you. Demand that they hear everything you have to say. Their ability to accurately diagnose your problem and provide you with the care you need depends on that. Make sure your advocate understands this and is willing to help you ensure that this happens. Insist that they take their time with you, that they are doing the best to get as much information as they can from you based on your symptom list, and that all your questions are answered in your initial consultation. Be courteous but firm. This is your life, and you need all the accurate information you can get.

Nothing about depression is easy, but it is not impossible to treat. I have presented you with a considerable amount of information to increase your understanding of this debilitating condition, how it affects your life, and what you can begin to do to turn things around. Now, it is up to you to begin the process of efficiently communicating your concerns to others. Make sure your advocate is interested in helping you and has the time to spend with you to make that happen. Then, together, you can begin the process of identifying the professionals who are going to help you change your world.

⏱ Time to Take Action

1. Be absolutely sure that you want to do the work that is necessary to address the depression that has so drastically affected your life. Then, make your decision to start your plan.

2. Identify your advocate, that support person who is going to help you identify the professionals you need to include in your professional network.

3. Make an appointment with your primary care physician and with a professional counselor. Your doctor may provide medicine to alleviate problems, but to learn how to make necessary life changes, a professional counselor is essential.

4. Remember not to focus solely on the end goal. That will only intimidate and overwhelm you. Take it step by step. Just identify your advocate, compile your personal symptom list, and make an appointment with your physician and a counselor. That is enough for now.

Driving It Home

The life thief has the appearance of a monster that has all the resources it needs to destroy your life. This, however, does not need to be the case. Typically, bullies, beasts, and monsters thrive because the fear they create, and the paralysis they instill keeps you stuck in a dark, foreboding world. Knowledge, and the understanding of what to do with it, gives you the tools you need to shine light where there was darkness. Identifying people who can help and putting the initial steps of your plan in place can mark the beginning of a new and healthy life.

YOUR DECLARATION IS: *Nothing is going to stop me. I am going to rise above the pain that has defined me.*

Onward

Moving past depression is all about moving forward. Unfortunately, we all have events in our lives that have caused pain for us and that may still be exerting their influence as we attempt to move forward. Before you do move forward, it is important to settle the past. In the next chapter, we will discuss leaving the past behind you.

CHAPTER 11

Leaving the Past in the Past: Forgiveness and Learning to Feel Worthy

There is no moving forward while you're looking back. Forgive yourself and see the world that is waiting for you.

PROCESSES TO EMPLOY: Brutal Honesty, I Over E, Present/Understand/Fix, Slowing Down Life's Pace, Internal Focus, Fact-Finding, Forgiveness, Settling Past Issues, Trust

YOU CAN'T GO FORWARD WHEN YOU ARE looking back. Everything in your life is happening in the moment you are living in, and it is always moving forward. Depression, with the negative energy it produces, can cause you to focus your attention on what has happened in the past and all the negative emotion surrounding those people and events. When this happens, your opinion of yourself, others in your world, and the world itself, can take on a drastically negative perspective.

Sometimes, your past can occupy intellectual and emotional space in your life that should be reserved for present events. When this happens, it can cause rumination, obsessive thinking, self-esteem issues, shame and guilt, depressed mood, and, at times, hopelessness that can have you questioning your desire to continue living. Examples of how your past can interfere with your present well-being are old family and relationship issues that didn't turn out well, past failures, childhood trauma, anger toward others you feel may have hurt you, and guilt or shame because you may have hurt someone or let them down.

It is hard to move forward when you feel as though you are anchored to the negative energy caused by events in your past. You already know how much energy depression and the often-accompanying anxiety can consume in your life. Each day, many of depression's symptoms such as sleep, diet, and intellectual and emotional pressures can leave us with only so much energy to use for what is happening that day. When some of that energy is diverted to reliving past events and the emotional pain they may have caused, it deprives you of the precious resources you must use to battle your life thief and live a happy life.

ALL HANDS ON DECK

If you decide to put your energies into a healthy life plan, there is no room for the gut-wrenching and paralyzing rumination on past relationships and events. You need as much energy as you can muster to get healthy and live your life happily. That life thief of yours is deeply connected to your past, and it understands how to dredge up events that do nothing but bring you down and cause you pain.

Past events must be released if you are going to break the chains that bind you to the depression monster. All your energy and resources must be applied to your movement forward, away from the debilitating issues of the past, and securely focused on what you need to do to restore yourself to a happy, productive life—it's all hands on deck! To move forward, you need to focus all available energy to making your plan come alive and defeat this life-ravaging thief.

FORGIVENESS AS A WAY TO SEVER THE CRIPPLING TIES

The pain associated with past events and the people involved in them can be difficult to let go of. At times, especially when guilt and anger are part of the event, you may not want to let them go just yet.

There are times when you feel you need to settle the score or that your victimization based on these events gives you a rational reason to remain in your dark, depressive world. This type of thinking is exactly what the thief looks for. Anything that can pull you away from the positive power that is available to you is a welcome addition to the beast's diabolical toolbox. I am going to give you the formula to leave the past in the past and move forward.

In *The Fix Yourself Handbook*, I offer a chapter on forgiveness as a way to leave the past behind you. In that context, I discussed forgiving yourself first. When you do, you learn the art of forgiveness, and you can apply it to those people and events that plague your life as you attempt to move forward. Forgiveness doesn't apply only to people in your life who may have hurt you or caused you pain. Forgiveness also has to do with those feelings of guilt, shame, and lack of accountability to yourself or others. It is important to put those issues to rest before you move forward.

Attempting to move forward without putting closure on past issues, whether they belong to you or others, can cause you to be intellectually and emotionally weighed down by them. It is difficult to attempt to build a new and exciting life when you feel as though you do not deserve it or if you are angry about or fixated on something someone else has done to you. Depression can keep you locked in the past with your mind inundated by people and events who you may have hurt or let down or who may have done the same to you.

In Chapter 3, I discussed those symptoms that apply to depression. One of those is thoughts of failure, guilt, and shame. As your feelings about yourself worsen, you may perceive yourself as a failure, and now feelings of failure, guilt and shame take over your world. This is where your internal language changes and you talk to yourself in terms that range from mildly depressed to downright abusive. It is also when you feel the strong need to avoid other people.

It is so interesting to see how the symptoms can not only overlap but also lead into each other. When you are experiencing thoughts of failure, guilt, and/or shame, your internal language will be negative. You begin to avoid other people, since you either are angry with them or you feel as though you are not good enough to be with them. This feeling becomes generalized, and you may find yourself avoiding people routinely. Consider this example.

Roger That

Roger is forty-two years old, divorced, and has worked on a construction team for fifteen years. He shows up to work every day and is a valuable employee. He owns his home and has a small group of close friends. His personal life is an unhappy one. Roger does not speak to his ex-wife, and his relationships with his son and daughter are strained. Roger holds on to old issues, doesn't forgive people who he feels caused him pain, and, as a result, stays away from creating any new intimate relationships. He has been seeing a woman for the past three years, but he keeps it casual and at arm's length. He has no intention of putting himself in a position to be hurt again.

Roger's anger has kept him in what he defines as a secure distance from others who could become much closer to him. While he is angry at those he feels have caused him problems, he is not looking at his own responsibility in those relationships. His anger has isolated him, and his ability to move forward has been severely compromised by his decision to not forgive and move on.

Pain Buddies

It is important to begin to let go of those past hurts so that you may embrace the new life you are building. It is a good idea to share your concerns with your advocate or anyone else you feel could help you with this process. Let's take a look at the initial steps you can take to move past those issues that may affect your forward progress.

It is so important to remove this negative energy from your world. The life thief holds its victims prisoner, not only to the physical the pain it causes but also to emotional pain that makes it so difficult to live a happy and productive life. Depression, the result of neurotransmitter imbalance and all the symptoms that it causes, changes the way you feel about yourself. You firmly believe that you are not a good person, that you have caused pain for yourself and other people, that you cannot be forgiven, and that you will remain and its dark and empty world.

The truth of the matter is that everyone makes mistakes. Everyone does things that hurt themselves and others around them. We all have our own flaws and imperfections, and though we all need to be accountable for our actions, we also need to be treated with compassion, to be forgiven for what we may have done, and to live a happy and positive life. You should never be forced to live a life sentence for making a few mistakes. You deserve to be treated with respect, and you need to forgive yourself for past wrongdoings.

Oh, but the life thief has a different plan. That dastardly little sneak is an expert at wrapping your symptoms around each other and forcing you to lose perspective about the events in your life. So, instead of simply feeling guilt and shame for what you have done, you are now losing interest or pleasure in doing things; feeling down, depressed, or hopeless; having trouble falling or staying asleep, or sleeping too much; feeling tired or having little energy; struggling with poor appetite, overeating, or considerable weight changes; feeling bad about yourself; being consumed by thoughts of failure or guilt; struggling to concentrate on things or making decisions; and may even be grappling with suicidal thoughts.

What began as a simple rumination over a past event has now grown into a multi-symptom monster. I use this example to show you that your symptoms have a way of growing together, and one of the reasons people with depression have a difficult time addressing one symptom is that it may attach itself to several others. You may be focusing on your guilt, shame, and horrible feelings about yourself regarding some past event, and while you are consciously putting your energy there, all those other little symptoms are making it that much more difficult for you to let go of those past pains.

This is such an important point to understand. This is also why we look at depression as a personalized condition. This allows us to address those symptoms and how they wrap around each other to help create your life on a personal level. So how do you forgive yourself when you are feeling so bad about what has happened, but all those symptoms in your life stand in the way of letting things go?

THE BASIC PLAN

- You cannot and will not do this alone. You will need the help of your advocate or someone you trust with your past information. If you have identified a counselor, this is a good time to bring this person into your personal world. They have the skills to guide you through this.

- With your advocate, go through every detail of those past situations. Try to leave none out. If you are going to let go of past pain, it is important to leave no emotional stone unturned. Unaddressed details tend to interfere with the process of forgiving yourself. This is where a counselor, someone who can help you work through these parts of the plan, comes in. Share those details you have discussed with your advocate with your counselor.

- If you and your counselor feel as though you caused someone pain, it is important to try to make amends with that person. You cannot control what they will do or say. However, you need to know that you did everything in your power to alleviate the pain a past situation may have caused.

- Your movement forward can commence when you feel as though amends have been made, facts are in order, and you have a plan to make sure those things don't happen again. Talk to your counselor about formulating that plan.

- If you feel others have behaved in a way that hurt you and you have a difficult time letting go of that pain, use the same format. Compile all the details in order and discuss the way you need to proceed with your counselor.

This last point is important: You are doing what you can to move forward. Stop using self-punishment to address what you have done. You do not need to emotionally flog yourself here. We all make mistakes, and you are part of that *we*. Put the facts in order, have a plan to ensure that it does not happen again, and then let it go. Sometimes, letting it go means going over the facts several times with your counselor. Remember, your mind under the influences of depression is not always efficient when it comes to information processing.

As you can see, when it comes to attempting to forgive yourself, the line between what you have done and who you are can become very blurred. Once again, depression is not who you are; it is a condition you have. It causes so many different things to happen, and it is important that you understand that having done these things is not an indicator of who you are. They are simply mistakes you made, and there is a way to move past them.

The life thief will do its best to keep you in it's dark and hopeless prison. You, however, are learning to understand that this is not who you are, and it is not the way things need to stay. Forgiving yourself and letting go of the past is another way of saying, "This is not who I am. These things either happened or became worse because of a condition I have." That condition either caused the problem or caused you to behave in a way that you could not understand and had no way of correcting. That changes now. You are not alone, and you are beginning to understand the nature of the life thief. Be willing to review the information you have gathered and do your best to forgive yourself. Doing so will open the doors to a new world full of that positive energy you have always been looking for.

⏱ Time to Take Action

1. Present the information in this chapter to your advocate, and let that person know that you want to review the necessary facts.

2. Make a list of those people and events in your past which you believe may be causing you to feel guilt or shame.

3. Make a list of anyone you feel may have caused you past pain that may be affecting the way you feel today.

4. If you have not made an appointment with the professional counselor, it is time to do so. Very often, working through past pain is more efficiently accomplished with the assistance of someone who is skilled in helping people through this process. Remember, this is something you cannot do alone, nor should you have to.

5. Involve your counselor in resolving past pain from your life and developing a plan to move forward.

6. Discuss what to do with each of these lists with your counselor. In some cases, you will be making amends. In other cases, you may need to discuss what to do to let go of those painful circumstances.

 **DRIVING IT HOME**

Learning to let go of your past gives you access to a new freedom that can become an invaluable part of the life you are trying to create. Past pain tends to muddy the waters going forward. Creating the new positive life you have been looking for requires clarity of thought and vision. It is so important to understand how to move forward and to be free of those past pains and the murky waters they can create. Forgiving yourself for what may have occurred at the hands of the life thief is essential in creating your new life and all the freedom that comes with it.

YOUR DECLARATION IS: *I will forgive myself and others, and I will live free and happy!*

 ONWARD

We are now moving into the most important part of your depression treatment plan. In the next chapter, we will start putting the plan in motion, beginning on the physical level. We will turn our attention to getting your body healthy enough to move past your depression and to begin to live that happy life you want to create.

CHAPTER 12

Putting Your Plan in Motion: It All Starts with Getting Your Body Healthy

Break free from the unhealthy ways of the past. Being kind to your body is the first step that can help define the rest of your life.

PROCESSES TO EMPLOY: Brutal Honesty, I Over E, Present/Understand/Fix, Slowing Down Life's Pace, Internal Focus, Fact-Finding, Life on Life's Terms, Journey Living, Keeping Life Simple

IN CHAPTER 3, I BEGAN DISCUSSING THE RELATIONSHIP between your body and your mind. I also explained how depression is primarily a physical disorder stemming from the imbalance in neurotransmitter production in your body. The correlation between physically unhealthy lifestyles and incidences of depression is quite high. The simple rule is that the healthier your body is, the more difficult it is for the life thief to do its dastardly deeds. This is not to say that healthy people cannot be depressed people. My point is to help you understand that, in fighting depression, a healthy body is a marvelous advantage.

Before I discuss making yourself healthier, it is important to understand what happens when depression dictates the way you take care of your body. If you refer back to Chapter 3 where I discussed the symptoms of depression in detail, you will note that many of them have to do with the effects depression has on your body. Some of those symptoms include a poor diet, lack of exercise, motivation issues, poor sleep schedule, low energy, using accelerants to feel better, self-harm, fatigue, and mood swings.

In Chapter 11, I noted that symptoms can overlap each other, making depression more difficult to diagnose, causing you to feel even worse, and making your depression more challenging to treat. Now think about what happens when your body becomes weakened at the hands of depression and the symptoms are overlapping each other, often attacking at the same time. *Depression attacks you physically first, then moves through your emotions, and finally attacks your mind.* It only makes good sense to give your body everything it needs to be as strong as it can be in this war against the life thief.

The criteria for a healthy body includes good nutrition, regular exercise, avoiding harmful habits, and seeking medical assistance when necessary. Pay special attention to the food you put in your body and understand that, as a physical entity, your body needs regular exercise to keep it healthy. You also need to avoid harmful habits like overeating, substance abuse, and physical harm. It also makes good sense to recognize and make good decisions for your physical health and to seek medical help if and when necessary.

If you are suffering from depression, you know that your body does not feel as good as it should. You may be tired, have aches and pains, and the systems in your body, based on poor neurotransmitter production, will not be operating at optimal levels. The question is, do you want to continue to live your life at the mercy of the life thief?

Interestingly, in my more than four decades of counseling, when people present their list of depression-related symptoms and concerns, aside from feeling down and out and mental/emotional concerns, the third most prevalent complaint relates to the way people feel physically. Though physical ailments rank number three on the list, if you look closely, both mood swings and that down-and-out feeling are closely tied to the way you feel physically. Fewer people say they feel down and out or they are experiencing mood swings when their bodies are healthy.

People will often do anything but take care of their bodies when it comes to taking care of their depression. They will try medicine, they will try all kinds of trending approaches, and they will talk about their symptoms, trying to alleviate them at the intellectual level first. As I have reiterated since Chapter 1, you really need to start with your body, since neurotransmitter production is at the root of everything you are feeling. So, let's start with our healthy eating plan. I will make it simple and to the point so you can incorporate into your life with just a little effort.

MY HEALTHY BODY: THE PLAN

Nutrition

Before I proceed with information about good nutrition, let's do a little primer about the gustatory system (the sense of taste). Taste is the perception stimulated when a substance in the mouth reacts chemically with taste receptor cells located on taste buds in the oral cavity, mostly on the tongue. Each taste bud contains 50 to 100 taste receptor cells. Taste receptors in the mouth sense the five basic tastes: sweetness, sourness, saltiness, bitterness, and savoriness. These five tastes are distinct from one another, so depending on your taste buds and their connection to your brain, you will have a preference for particular foods, and these commonly provide more pleasure for you when you are eating.

Good nutrition is all about putting the right things in your body, in the right amounts, and at the right times. People like to eat what they like, in the amounts they like, and when they like. Many people enjoy that full feeling in their stomachs and will eat until they reach that point. As I mentioned in Chapter 3, it is your brain that determines when you are full, so retraining your brain to reinterpret that process makes sense. This is how it happens. First, eat slowly. This gives your brain enough time to interpret what is entering your stomach. Second, give your brain an understanding of what nutrition is. You do this by slowly phasing out all those comfort foods that lead to weight gain and other physical problems. You should also remove accelerants like caffeine and energy drinks from your diet. Caffeine can raise the anxiety level and lead to depressive crashes, while energy drinks, often packed with caffeine, are also high in sugar. Sugar can also cause depressive crashes. Oh, and by the way, not everyone feels the effects of caffeine the same way, and even though you may not feel the acceleration, your brain can adapt to it, and remember, there is that mental part of depression. So, it makes sense to go slow on the caffeine.

Comfort foods are a major problem when it comes to depression. People who suffer from depression will do anything to feel better. One can feel better, albeit for short periods of time, by introducing a food loaded with flavor enhancers that immediately provide a relief from the depression. Changing your diet really has to do with training your brain. One of the brain's more adaptive processes is something we call habit formation. This is your brain adapting to the choices you make, and as it does, it provides less resistance to choices that may not be so good for you.

In terms of nutrition, if you keep on putting comfort foods into your body, your brain will adjust, understand that these foods please you, and motivate you to continue seeking and eating those foods. To retrain your brain, you can gradually (within a month or six weeks) reduce your intake of comfort foods and a gradually introduce healthy foods. Start by reducing the amount of comfort foods you eat. Comfort foods tend to be high in carbohydrates, sugar, and salt. Try to get away from fast foods, prepared foods that are made via your microwave, and foods with flavor enhancers, colorings, and chemical additives. Whole foods are your best bet.

Typically, adults should consume around 60 to 80 grams of protein per day. You can get your protein from meet (animal or plant based) if you choose to eat then, or you can introduce protein shakes and protein bars into your diet. Protein bars are a good substitute for candies, since they tend to be sweet. Do try to select protein bars that are low in carbohydrates and sugars. Protein synthesis is a key element in fighting depression, so getting enough protein in your diet every day helps fight depression and helps supply energy to your muscles. This is advantageous to you when you begin an exercise plan, as you will see shortly.

The life thief loves to introduce refined carbohydrates into your diet. They cause weight gain and are almost always involved in overeating. Those cakes, cookies, chips, and other quick comfort fixes have low nutritional value and are high in calories. Also, no food has more artificial ingredients and chemical enhancers than carbohydrates. So not only are you putting substances in your body that can cause weight gain, but they are also full of those substances that have drastic negative effects on your body such as diabetes, gout, high blood pressure, etc.

Try to get your carbohydrates from vegetables and fruits. If you don't like to eat them with your meals, put them in a protein shake. In some cases, you can buy the shakes that include these nutrients to help create a healthy meal supplement. Balancing your diet is the first step in getting your body healthy. It is something you have control over, and little by little, it can help give you more of what you need to fight your depression.

Keep in mind that you do not have to eliminate comfort foods from your diet all together. There is nothing wrong with a little cheat here and there. Just try not to make it the basis for your nutritional plan. If you would like to go more in depth when it comes to your nutrition, a nutritionist would be a nice addition to your professional network. In the meantime, here is a simple recipe for a nutritious protein shake. You can include this in your reading plan as a supplement to a healthy diet.

MY HEALTHY PROTEIN SHAKE

INGREDIENTS: 12 ounces dairy or nondairy milk with at least 20 grams of protein

1 scoop protein powder

1/2 cup of fruit

1/2 cup fruit juice, water, or green tea

1 scoop of super green powder (about an ounce) vegetable juice (about 4 ounces)

DIRECTIONS: In a blender, combine all the ingredients. Blend on high until smooth and frothy, about 1 to 2 minutes.

There is one very important last point about nutrition. Very often, people who are depressed and not practicing good nutrition tend to become dehydrated or, at the very least, do not hydrate their bodies well. One of the most important practices to support good nutritional habits is to stay hydrated. Try to finish the drink even if you were taking small sips during the course of the day.

The average adult human's body is made up of almost 70 percent water. Water helps keep a normal body temperature, lubricates and cushions joints, protect your spinal cord and other sensitive tissues, and helps rid the body of wastes through urination, perspiration, and bowel movements. Most important, it has a profound impact on the way the brain performs. Try to stay hydrated.

Exercise

Oh, no, there's that E word that so many people despise! Remember, what you give your brain is what your brain adjusts to and then tries to keep you doing—or not doing. When I talk about exercise, I am not talking about mountain climbing or swimming across the English Channel. Again, it is important for you to retrain your brain. Depression causes it to become used to a sedentary and purposeless way of living. You want to reverse that.

The exercise plan is simple. Get off the couch and start becoming a bit more active. Start by introducing about 30 minutes of exercise into your daily routine. Try to do this at the same time every day and try not to miss a day. It could be walking, riding your bike, or using exercise equipment if you have some. At the very least, program some mild or calisthenics, or you can begin to do some of the fundamental yoga exercises.

The benefits of including exercise in your daily routine are twofold. First, it breaks the sedentary routine your mind has adjusted to. We know the unmotivated lifestyle is a key factor in depressive symptomology. You want to change that, and you can do that by introducing short periods of gentle exercise to get you started. The other advantage is that it helps you become a healthier person, and you need that to help you fend off your life thief. It doesn't matter what type of exercise you do; you just want to get started with something, and you want to be consistent about it.

If you can, invite a friend to exercise with you. Sometimes depression drains your motivation making it difficult to maintain an exercise plan, so having an exercise buddy can increase your motivation and may help to keep you consistent with the plan. If possible, as your mind and body adjust to the physical changes, increase the scope and duration of your exercise sessions.

Avoiding Harmful Habits

While including all this good food and exercise in your plan, you also want to avoid all those harmful things you did or may still be doing that can exacerbate the depression symptoms. The best way to start this is to establish a daily schedule that is healthy and consistent. Get up at the same time every day. Incorporate a good diet, exercise, and a few items of interest. Get the abusive substances out of your diet. Avoid too much time on social media, on your cell phone, just watching movies and TV, or even reading time loaded with comfort foods. That habit formation I discussed earlier is what causes your brain to pair good choices with not-so-good choices. For example, reading is a good thing; reading with a bag of cookies and a soda next to you is not so good.

Often, people with depression tend to look for comfort items. Tobacco can be one of those. It is unhealthy for your body to begin with, but it also creates highs and lows in your brain. Though you may not feel any euphoria when you smoke a cigarette, you will note that you feel better after you smoke one. That is because cigarette you are smoking addresses the withdrawal from the last cigarette. It is creating highs and lows that you do not need. Marijuana is the new substance savior, but make no mistake about it, it is a drug. It does create highs and lows, and contrary to popular belief, it can be addictive. Be careful with this one. Vaping is also viewed by some with people as safe, or at least not as bad as smoking. The mist that vaping produces was never meant for your lungs, and for many, it is still delivering substances that can either heightened depression symptoms, or, at times, cause anxiety. This is another one to be very careful about.

In short, try to remove anything in your life that can have negative consequences. It is common for people to say that those who advise healthy choices are trying to take all the good stuff out of life and that they want to hold on to at least a few vices. That decision is yours. Do know, however, that anything you do that works against your body and your mind will have negative consequences, and you must be ready to deal with those. It seems a bit contrary to say you want to feel better when you cling to those things that don't make you feel better in the long run. Try to be consistent.

Seeking Medical Assistance When Necessary

There are three kinds of people in the world when it comes to getting help with a medical problem: those who react quickly and call the doctor for almost everything, those who give a symptom proper attention and call a physician if necessary, and those who refuse any type of medical help altogether. When it comes to facing depression, you should staunchly avoid becoming a member of the last group.

When the information you have compiled suggests the need for medical intervention, you need to follow through. This might mean consulting a physician to either treat something you know is a problem or, at the very least, to determine whether it is a problem. Remember, one of the prime symptoms of depression is procrastination and not following through. If you are having trouble with this one, talk to your symptoms over with your advocate to determine if scheduling an appointment with your physician is necessary. Let your trusted people help you. Don't avoid medical help when you need it. Doing so amounts to nothing less than feeding the life thief.

A healthy body is a major player in the creation of a healthy mind and healthy emotions. Those people not suffering from depression may have it just a bit easier when it comes to maintaining a healthy body, but you cannot use that as an excuse to not take care of your own. Having a healthy body is the first step in removing depression from your life. Those who embrace the concept of a healthy body will eventually feel the rewards that come with being strong enough physically to wage war against a demonic force that has, for so long, taken over your life.

TIME TO TAKE ACTION

1. Inform your advocate that you are going to make changes to become healthier physically. That person should be involved from the beginning to help you make the right decisions.

2. Discuss your diet plan with your physician or nutritionist and begin to remove the foods that cause weight gain, mood swings, and lethargy. Then, begin introducing good foods into your diet. It makes sense to create a list of the foods you want to remove and those you want to add.

3. Discuss your exercise plan based on your own physical condition and talk about what you want to include in your plan to get started. If you are used to periods of exercise, you may be at a more intermediate level. If, however, you are a beginner, then you can start with slower steps, like walking for about thirty minutes. You may need to consult your doctor on this one if there are physical concerns about what exercise is safe for you.

4. Make a list of those harmful things you may be doing, like substance abuse and smoking. Be honest about this list. Then, if necessary, and with the advice of your physician, begin to remove those habits from your life.

5. Journaling is a very smart addition to both your nutritional plan and your exercise. This helps you keep track of what needs to stay, what needs to go, and what needs to be added. It also helps you track your progress.

6. Be willing to seek the accurate information you need to make decisions, and then act on those decisions in timely fashion, whether they are lifestyle decisions or those medical decisions discussed earlier.

 DRIVING IT HOME

Your life has been inundated with the darkness the life thief has brought into it. You have been desperate for a plan that can make you healthier and happier and remove depression and its symptoms from your life. It all starts with getting your body healthy. Remember what I said in Chapter 1: Many people attempt to alleviate depression by thinking their way through it and coming up with changes they believe are based on removing memories and present circumstances from their lives. While these all need to be done, it starts with your body. Too many people try to address their decision without proper nutrition and an exercise plan. Very few succeed. Start by making some improvements. Getting healthy is the first step in creating a foundation for the changes your body will need to make to say goodbye to the life thief.

YOUR DECLARATION IS: *I will become healthy, and I will make it difficult for the life thief to be part of my world.*

 ONWARD

Now that you have the information you need to start getting your body healthier, I will turn to retraining your brain. Just as proper nutrition and exercise can retrain your brain to become healthier on a physical level, retraining your brain intellectually is a key component in banishing depression from your life. In the next chapter, we are going to discuss how to bring control back into your intellectual command center.

CHAPTER 13

Retraining Your Brain: Bringing Control Back to Your Intellectual Command Center

Repetition over time: it's the recipe that retrains your brain and creates the pathways to intellectual freedom.

PROCESSES TO EMPLOY: Brutal Honesty, I Over E, Present/Understand/Fix, Slowing Down Life's Pace, Internal Focus, Fact-Finding, Incremental Forward Movement, Sustained Learning, Time/Energy Management, Humility, Risk-Taking, Trust

IN CHAPTER 12, I GAVE YOU AN ABUNDANCE of information regarding how to get yourself back on track physically. We discussed the profound effect of reduced neurotransmitter production on your body and what you can do to strengthen yourself to fend off the assaults of the life thief. In this chapter, we turn our attention to how this imbalance in chemical production affects your brain. Keep in mind that the brain is responsible to either initiate or assist the body and its various systems and organs in every operation the body performs.

One of those operations, and arguably the most important operation, is that it organizes all your thought processes. In Chapter 6, I presented a basic overview of how neurotransmitters work. To keep our flow in this chapter constant, I will present a quick recap: A neurotransmitter is a chemical substance that is released at the end of a nerve fiber by the arrival of a nerve impulse that, by spreading this impulse more widely across the synapse or junction, causes the transfer of the impulse to another nerve fiber, a muscle fiber, or some other structure. So this chemical movement from nerve to nerve or nerve to other structures allows your brain to think and process information efficiently.

Your brain learns. It also relearns. For you to continually adjust to and transition through all of life's little bumps and curves, your brain must perform its learning and relearning processes repeatedly and consistently. Learning is a matter of repetition over time. Only in rare instances does your brain receive a single information item and learn it immediately. It may memorize it and store it for a short period of time for rapid usage, but to efficiently repeat the behavior as it was presented and turn that behavior into a learned process that can be applied routinely, repeated presentations over a period of time are necessary.

THE LIFE THIEF AT WORK

That sneaky little life thief is aware of your brain's need to constantly learn and relearn. So in that hamster-on-a-wheel, groundhog day way of living it trained your brain to experience, over and over, and all those uncomfortable symptoms I discussed in Chapter 2. Your inability to move past those symptoms and your tendency to repeat them each day provides the fertile learning environment for the life thief to teach your brain to think and behave and in a way that is dark and depressed. Soon, *the combination of neurotransmitter imbalance and the lessons your brain learns by repetitive depressed activity produce that condition we call depression.*

To illustrate, let's look at an example. Richard is a thirty-five-year-old construction worker. Both of his parents suffered from depression, and there is a history of substance abuse on the paternal side of the family. In addition, an uncle on his mother's side committed suicide, and several relatives on each side of the family are taking antidepressants. Genetically, Richard is predisposed to depression. In addition, Richard lived with his parents until he was nineteen. Richard has struggled with depression since he was a teenager but refuses to go on antidepressants. He feels this is something he can take care of on his own.

Richard's wife, Adele, has noticed that he has become increasingly detached from her and their three children. He is spending more time alone and leaving the house rarely, except to go to church and to work. Richard has begun to consume a bit more alcohol, though he is neither abusive to his family nor is his drinking what she would describe as significant. She notes a reduction in his social life, and he is spending more time in front of the TV.

In a recent conversation, Adele got Richard to talk about his childhood, and as she did, Richard began to realize that his behavior was beginning to resemble that of his father's. During his father's depression, he would isolate, drink more, see friends less, and dwell on old issues. So, what's happening to Richard?

We know that Richard is a product of two depressed people and that he lived in an environment where he saw the effects of depression in the way they both behaved. What we see here is the marriage of Richard's biology and his environment. Being the son of two depressed parents and his lowered rate of neurotransmitter production may have set the stage for his depression. However, something else is in the picture: learned behavior. Even though Richard was able to hold depression at bay up to this point in his life, the combination of his genetics and the learned behaviors he adopted from his parents caused his depression to become more pronounced. He was using his father's methods to live with the thief.

WHY CAN'T I?

Nothing about depression is more frustrating than knowing what you need to do, wanting to do it, and not being able motivate yourself to make it happen. You know that you want or need to get something done and you know that you are capable of doing it, but you just can't get things started. No matter what you do, even the simplest actions seem like monumental tasks. Not only are you faced with what seems like an inability to perform something that is very simple, you are also feeling like a failure. Intellectually and emotionally, it is easy to become disheartened.

You know your brain works because you can feel it receiving information from all your senses. It is not like you are brain dead with absolutely no thoughts going through your mind. In fact, very often, there are too many thoughts going through your head. You know the information is there, but you cannot seem to understand and interpret it. This is where you begin to doubt your intellectual abilities and, ultimately, your sanity. This is also where your opinion of yourself takes a huge hit, and you begin to think that this depressed person is the person you are.

Depression attacks you intellectually, physically, emotionally, and spiritually every day. Unfortunately, your brain adjusts to this training program, and it becomes a routine way of living for you. Your brain begins to interpret the reduction in functioning as your own personal norm. Soon, you adjust to the norm and stop challenging yourself to interpret and act upon the information, knowing it would probably produce nothing but failure. Your opinion of yourself becomes a function of this negative learning curve. You, yourself, are becoming negative, self-sabotaging, and stuck in an intellectual wasteland—the thief's wasteland.

There is, however, one important item you may not have considered: Though your brain, based on your neurotransmitter imbalance, is not operating according to healthy parameters, it is still healthy enough to accept training. It has been doing so all along, albeit with negative guidance. With the right program, your brain can still respond to a new training program if you are willing to take the time to provide it with positive energy. There is a correlation between getting your body and mind healthier and a reduction in depressive symptoms. However, this does require improving your physical health and retraining your brain to work with positive energy.

THE RETRAINING PROCESS

Looking back at our friend Richard, his brain not only suffered from imbalanced chemical production, but also from the effects of a long and arduous training process at the hands of the life thief. His brain learned how to behave with depression as his own personal norm. This is an example of that learning over time I mentioned earlier. Depressed neurological activity causes your brain to continue to experience energy infusion, but unfortunately, it is negative energy. So, we are going to flip the switch on our learning-over-time process and begin to infuse your brain with positive energy.

The human mind receives and then interprets energy as positive or negative charges. These changes come from the energy you receive from your senses and from your own internal language. Depression can have a significant impact the way you interpret that energy. It all depends on what your brain is receiving in terms of neurotransmitter production and how you work with it on any given day. The question when it comes to retraining the brain is, can a new training program designed to strengthen your body and your mind have a positive impact on the way your brain operates? To the point, if you have depression, can you retrain your brain to more efficiently receive and interpret information and provide you with the energy you need to act upon it? The answer is yes, but it is a little more involved in the training process.

THE RETRAINING STEPS

Medication

For some people, prescription drugs are going to be part of their treatment plan. In such cases where the neurotransmitter imbalance is significant, it may be important to "jumpstart" the brain to eventually help the person's neurotransmitters function properly on their own. In almost every case, these medications take approximately two to three weeks to upload to clinical levels, at which time the person may or may not feel better. That depends on the person and the medication. For some people, these medications will be prescribed for life. For others, the amount of time can be significantly shorter, possibly a year or two, if not less.

Before you begin taking medication, however, you should begin working with a professional counselor to determine if you are able to work through the depression without medicine. This is certainly possible, but results vary from person to person. The basic rule for medication is to keep the dose as low as possible and to take as few medications as possible. If you and your counselor feel it may be a good idea to take an antidepressant, make an appointment with your primary care physician and get the necessary blood analysis done. As mentioned, genetic testing is also advised to determine which medications would be most advantageous for you and which ones to avoid. I always try to make medication a last resort, but in cases of severe depression and the possibility of self-harm, it may become part of the treatment plan a little earlier. I'll be discussing medications in detail in Chapter 16.

Dietary Changes

I have already discussed the advantages of a healthy nutritional plan to assist you in strengthening your body. Just as your mind adjusts to the training it receives from depressed activity caused by neurotransmitter imbalance, your body also adjusts to a poor diet and learns how to live with what you are feeding it. In short, it learns to function as an unhealthy body. Beginning to change the way you eat—including the right foods, in the right amounts, at the right times, and reducing your intake of unhealthy foods—represents a healthy way of retraining your body. Your body will react much quicker to the training program than your mind, and it will assist your mind in accepting the parameters of its own training program. One hand is indeed washing the other here.

Exercise

I touched on the advantages of an exercise program in Chapter 12.

However, there is one additional point that can go a long way in assisting you in your new training process. You may be familiar with the concept of the "runner's high" typically associated with long-distance running. After a period of running, the increase in chemicals like dopamine, serotonin, and endorphins resulting from an extended period of physical exercise causes some people to feel euphoric. We now know that including periods of exercise in one's routine daily plan also has a positive impact on their neurotransmitter production. So, not only is exercise good for your body, it also helps your brain receive the chemicals it needs to operate efficiently. There's that mind-body connection again!

Counseling

In Chapter 11, I began to discuss how leaving your past in the past can be difficult and how including a program of professional counseling could be advantageous for you. In an extension of that chapter's advice, the very fact that depression produces intellectual and emotional deficits that make difficult for you to move forward, tells you that talking to someone who has an expertise in depression can be a wonderful addition your brain's retraining program. Depression causes you to think about yourself in negative and uncomplimentary terms. It trains your brain to believe that there is something wrong with you and that you may not be a good person.

As you retrain your mind and your body, it makes very good sense have someone help you retrain the way you think about and speak to yourself. Call it a positive energy guide. This is where you can put many old issues to rest, but also where you learn how to think, feel, and behave as a healthier person. Counseling can also help you reinforce other parts of the retraining program. In addition, it is so beneficial to talk with someone who understands the retraining process and knows how to help you with it. It's so much more efficient to have someone to guide you in the right directions, rather than continuously asking yourself "am I doing the right thing"? and not being able to answer the question.

Increased Social Contact

In Chapter 7, I discussed the feelings of being alone and the concept of aloneness at the hands of the life thief. You may now understand that, as a depressed person, the more time you spend alone, the more time that you are spending at the hands of your personal life thief. Learning how to spend time with other people, even in small safe places, can give you an opportunity to take a break from the beast's influence. Instead of listening to negative verbalizations about who you are and what you have become, you can lighten things up for a little while and program a temporary escape from the thief's "close your life off clutches." It is a system reset, even if just for a short period of time. It will also give you the understanding that people do enjoy your company and that you are not as abnormal as you thought.

Social interactions do not have to be included in your routine often, but you should spend a little time with other people in social situations on a regular basis—say, every other week or so to get things started. We talked about including your advocate or those people you trust in your life. That is a good idea, but I suggest opening up just a little more and being part of something that gets you back into the social flow. Make it safe, with people you trust, in the beginning, and then be willing to take a few social risks and do things with them that you typically might avoid. Socializing with others instead of your life thief is a huge positive retraining exercise for your brain.

Reduction of Negative Influencers

In Chapter 11, I discussed how the life thief encourages you to include negative components in your life. These are items like substance abuse, doing things that are harmful to your body like overeating and smoking, and anything that keeps you in a negative frame of mind. This is also where you try to reduce those quick-fix items that are nothing more than distractions from the depression but that do very little, if anything, to help you become a healthier person.

Let's call this cleansing the palate and creating space or positive growth and change. It is hard to move forward if you let those little negatives pull you back. Be willing to remove as many of those negative influencers as you can. By doing this, you are retraining your brain to take care of you, and self-care is a vital intellectual retraining strategy. Your advocate can help you make a list of these items, and you can present those to your counselor to help you remove them, or at the very least, reduce their impact in your life.

Positive Verbalizations

In Chapter 3, I began to discuss how or internal language can have a dramatic impact on the way you think and feel. Nothing in your world is more powerful when it comes to training your brain than the way you speak to yourself internally. It is hard to talk to yourself kindly when you do not feel good about yourself or when you think you are a failure. I'm not suggesting that you quickly turn it around and start saying beautiful things to yourself. Instead, begin this part of the program by first doing the best you can to stop the abusive language you are using to describe yourself and what is happening in your life.

The second part of this process is to replace those verbalizations with positive statements. You don't have to say "I love myself" just yet. However, you can begin to reinforce some of the good things you do, even if they are very small. You might say "I did a good job with that," or "I like the way this shirt looks on me." These sound like simple statements that will have no impact. However, like anything else in your life, if you do the little things over and over, they become the way you normally think and behave. That is, they retrain your brain to do things differently. When you can, begin to say things to yourself like "I am a good person, I just need to change a few things," you will be surprised how, over time, this simple but powerful linguistic change can alter the course of your life.

Pushing the Limits

In *The Fix Yourself Handbook*, I discussed the change monster and how so many people have such a difficult time with the concept of change. Pushing the limits means nothing more than instituting very small changes in your life. Those incremental forward movements I talk about really help to retrain your brain, since they remove some of the sticking spots in your life that can become toxic.

Depression can keep you stuck in that monotonous, self-defeating routine that keeps you at the mercy of the life thief as I discussed in Chapter 6. As yet another way to help you retrain your brain, try to break out of the monotony. Throw just a little change into your routine every day. You can start with simple things around the house. You can include some social events if possible, and even look at some of those little fears you have and maybe challenge a few.

For this step, it is a good idea to include your counselor and your advocate in the plan. Let them help you with a step by step plan to help you introduce small changes in your life. Your brain we'll begin to adjust not only to the small changes, but also to change as a routine part of your retraining process and the way you are learning to think.

All or Nothing

There is one important point about retraining your brain: You will do your best with your training program if you are willing to include everything I am presenting here. If you choose to omit one or more, expect less forward movement in your program. As you start your retraining program, I do strongly suggest you attempt to incorporate all of these components. You're not looking to negotiate some type of agreement with the life thief. Depression does not negotiate. The better plan is to attempt to annihilate it completely. You don't set your goals low on this one. The stronger you are willing to become, the more likely you are to remove the thief from your life. Decide how willing you are to include each of these components in your retraining program.

Get Help

The last point should be an obvious point. You are suffering with depression. Much of what you already tried has not worked. You are dealing with motivation and information interpretation issues, you tend to procrastinate, and you often do not follow through. Those are some of the depression symptoms that make it difficult to stick with this type of retraining program. So, do enlist the help of your advocate and your personal counselor. They are going to be instrumental in helping you understand what to do and to act on that information. They are also going to be there to reinforce what you are doing, and it's always nice to have that dedicated cheerleader who is going to give you a pat on the back when you need it. Do not do this alone. Let others be part of the process. Do not be afraid to ask for their help. Again, you are worth all the time it takes.

⏱ Time to Take Action

1. With an understanding that the brain is adaptable and therefore trainable, make the decision to take the necessary steps to retrain your brain to accept the positive changes it is capable of making.

2. You will need help with this part of the program. That is to be expected. Bring your advocate and anyone else you trust in your life close to support you as you make these changes.

3. Make a list of the first changes you want to make in each of the training steps presented above. Let your advocate, people your trust, and your counselor help you with this.

4. To initiate these changes, remember that you are making them in small increments. In each step, decide on one item from your list of that you want to change and how you want to make that happen. Move on to the next item when you are comfortable with the changes you have made. I will discuss more about how to make this part of the program practical and actionable in Chapter 18.

5. Slow and consistent is the way you want to begin the retraining program. No one makes any changes by biting off too much at one time or going too fast. Be easy on yourself, but be accountable to yourself, and don't stop.

6. Try not to skip any of the steps, because if you do, that makes it just a little more difficult for your brain to accept the training program you are putting in place.

7. Journaling about your retraining program makes good sense. Record the progress you are making with each component of the plan and any concerns you may have. Share this information with your counselor and your advocate.

8. Let the people who are helping you review your progress with you routinely. This helps you stay accountable, provides continued support, and helps you maintain your consistency in the program.

 ## Driving It Home

Nothing about depression is easy, but nothing about changing it is impossible. You can do anything you want to do with a viable plan to help you get there. Every good plan begins by removing the obstacles and problematic items that may hold you back. Try to remove those items from your life. You have been spinning your intellectual and emotional wheels for so long, searching for a program that can work for you. You now have one. Be willing to do the work, and make your personal program work for you. There is always help if you are willing to let other people in. It requires a bit of trust, but in the end, it might just help you see the light at the end of a life-changing tunnel.

YOUR DECLARATION IS: *I will embrace my program, retrain my brain, and begin to claim my new world!*

 ## Onward

In Chapters 12 and 13, I presented the information you need to start making changes physically and intellectually. The life thief has done its best to keep you stuck in a motionless and robotic way of life. In the next chapter, we will examine the benefits of getting into action and how it can help you change the way you live.

CHAPTER 14

Action, Action! The Benefits of a Body in Motion

Maintaining momentum is one of the most important strategies in defeating the life thief.

PROCESSES TO EMPLOY: Brutal Honesty, I Over E, Present/Understand/Fix, Slowing Down Life's Pace, Internal Focus, Fact-Finding, Risk-Taking, Incremental Forward Movement, Patience, One Day At A Time, Trust

THROUGHOUT OUR DISCUSSIONS, WE HAVE EXAMINED the life thief's devious strategy of keeping you unmotivated, confused, struggling to make decisions, and motionless, without direction. All of this has produced an actionless way of living. Though you can see much of what you want to do, even if you possess the ability to do it, you remain trapped in a void of lethargy, stuck in a world that seems to be going nowhere. The dark and depressed world is exactly where thief wants you to live. As long as you remain in this unmotivated, do-nothing world, your life thief remains in control, and you remain a prisoner, always under its oppressive influence.

If you could muster the energy and the motivation to act upon what your mind knows it wants to do, you could pierce depression's sinister armor and break free of its debilitating grasp. The imbalance in your body's chemical production, however, continues to breathe life into the monster, and you always seem to be at its unrelenting mercy. What if you could move past that sticking point and, even for brief moments of time, remove depression's life stealing cloak and breathe a little motivation in your gloomy world? It could be the beginning of a new way to live.

As I said in the last chapter, nothing about depression is good, but nothing about depression has to be permanent. Throughout this book, I have made it clear that progress is possible, but it needs to be a step-by-step process, one that could take some time to develop. I have also discussed taking the little steps, those minor advances that are so important. These minor movements forward are the little bridges that keep you moving in the right direction and toward eventual solutions to the problems depression causes. As you take the little steps and see glimpses of success, you grow more confident in your abilities to slowly move beyond the clutches of the life thief.

A CALL TO ACTION

Being in action is the antithesis to depression's unmotivated and sedentary way of living. As I previously discussed, depression keeps you locked in an unmotivated world, at times almost devoid of activity. Physically, your body acclimates itself to a motionless world with little movement and few goals. Intellectually, you become stifled and have difficulty interpreting information, making decisions, and putting those decisions into action. Emotionally, you beat yourself up, living each day with the near-certainty of impending doom.

One of the problems people encounter when attempting to work through depression is that you need to set goals and then attempt to achieve them immediately. When you are in the throes of depression, you will likely find it too difficult to make such strides. As a result, you define yourself as a failure and much of your forward movement stagnates. The problem is that no one moves from the starting point to the goal in a few easy steps. Depression can create an underlying state of desperation, and your mind firmly believes that it must accomplish something significant to convince you that you are worthy of your earthly existence. This, almost always, is a very damaging way to think and to live.

Setting goals can be a good thing. Goals give us a direction for our thoughts and actions, and once achieved, goals give us a sense of value and worth. This also provides a wonderful confidence boost. Under the life thief's depressive spell, however, attempting to move forward with grandiose goals, or even goals that require many steps, can be a difficult undertaking. This can be an intimidating venture and, at times, the source of demoralizing failures. You do want to move past the unmotivated, sedentary lifestyle and into something with a bit more productivity, so let's put the grandiose goals aside. In fact, let's even put aside the more complex forward movement—those little goals that require several to many steps—and let's simplify the procedure.

ACTION, SLOW AND STEADY

As I suggested in Chapter 13, the best way to move forward is in small, incremental steps. Your brain is not yet processing larger amounts of information, so I am going to keep this part of the program simple and easy to start. This doesn't require a complicated process that you will abandon quickly due to its complexity. I suggest these little steps to help introduce a healthier way of living into your daily routine. These are small changes, but changes nonetheless, and certainly changes you can work with. Try not to be overwhelmed, and again, take little steps, but be consistent.

I am going to present this process with a bit of a twist though. At this point in the program, I am not concerned with whether you are setting and accomplishing goals; that will come as we move deeper into the program. For now, the only thing I am concerned about is that you introduce a few periods of action into your day. Periods of action are any type of activity that calls for you to perform an endeavor, regardless of whether it meets a goal or accomplishes something you feel needs to be completed.

I am merely asking you to get up and do something. You could just get up and walk around. You might follow that by going out to get the mail, folding a few towels, wiping down the counters, or anything at all that makes you move. In the beginning, do not worry about assigning any intellectual value to the actions. They do not have to be planned, they don't have to be part of some goal you are trying to achieve, and they don't even have to be efficient. The only concern I have for you at this point is to get your body moving.

In Chapter 12, I discussed how exercise can help your body become healthier and make you more physically able to fend off the life thief, with the added advantage of neurotransmitter increase as a result of physical activity. I do want you to keep an exercise plan as part of your routine, but throughout the day, simply get up and do anything that keeps your body in motion. As the old adage goes, a body in motion stays in motion. Likewise, if you keep your body stagnant, you will remain stagnant. You want to do everything you can to work against the nature of the life thief, starting with small, incremental steps that can help to reverse depression's grip on you.

TO HAVE MEANING, OR NOT TO HAVE MEANING

When discussing seemingly meaningless actions, the people I counsel question the approach initially, saying that these actions do not seem to serve a purpose. Not everything we do must have a definable purpose. If you decide to take a walk at the end of your day, maybe around the block where you live or around a local park, there is no real intention behind the activity; you just decided that you wanted to do something to get your body in motion. Maybe you were getting restless at home, or maybe you decided to make it part of your exercise routine.

These little periods of action, which can range from thirty seconds to a few minutes, do not need an intended purpose. Try to get away from the notion that you are doing something ridiculous because you cannot do anything else. You are putting your body into action to lead to periods of time where your action *will* have an intended purpose, and those periods of time are going to be longer and more significant. However, you do need to start from the beginning. That means you need get your body acclimated to brief periods of activity.

If there is a goal here, it is simply to program activity into your life. The most significant time to begin these little periods of activity is when you do not want to do anything at all, because it is those times that make you feel worse about yourself. If you can do something small during one of these "I want to do nothing right now" times, you're actually working against the flow of your depression. *You are waging war against the life thief.* That, in and of itself, is huge.

Did you ever think that you could go from state of depression to a point where the depression was gone, and did you think you could do this in ten easy steps? In counseling, I would tell you that together we can defeat the life thief. However, I would also tell you that it is going to take us some time and that it is going to be a process. Everything I do with the people I counsel and in every program I write is the result of the processes that take you from where you are to where you want to be.

Those programs that preach getting you from places of pain and conflict to some type of wonderland where your love for yourself can immediately be found cannot and will never exist. They have all the trendy language, all the acronyms and programs that you must buy to convince you that, somehow, you are going to beat your demon with little to no work. There is *always* a process. It moves slowly, but it also moves consistently and provides wonderful little rewards along the way. In the end, you will not only beat your demon, but you will understand the processes that applies to addressing every component of your life as it presents itself.

Embrace the concept of little steps—those small, incremental forward movements. Get your body in motion. Have no concerns whatsoever about whether the actions you are taking will somehow bring you to some marvelous conclusion that will change your life. Do not be concerned about whether they are going to bring you out of your depression right now. Stay in the moment, keep your body in motion, do the smallest little things over and over again, and retrain your body to move from one that is fixed and sedentary to one that can embrace the little steps that will eventually lead to the higher-level processes in the program. You will need to start small to get to those more advanced parts of the program

Very little in your world will ever occur simply as a function of time passing. It is what you choose to do as time elapses that creates lasting changes. Begin the process of including little physical movements into your treatment plan. Use them in conjunction with your exercise program. Your mind, as strong as it is, wants to help you adapt to what you are attempting to change and turn that into a happy and productive way of living. Give the little steps time, stay committed, and give your body and your mind everything necessary to succeed.

TIME TO TAKE ACTION

1. Each day, include brief periods of action into what you are doing. It doesn't matter what you do. Just keep your body in motion, doing little things for as long and often as you can.

2. Try not to get caught up in whether these actions are relevant or important. They are simply intended to help you learn to keep your body acclimated to being in motion.

3. Let your advocate and/or your counselor know that you are incorporating these little movements into your process plan. They can help you initiate the process and keep it going.

4. Journaling about these little steps also make sense. You can either write down what you are doing or, since they are small and seemingly insignificant steps, you may just keep a tally of how many times you move into action each day. This will help you by giving you a visual look at the progress you are making.

5. Once your body accepts this small-step physical retraining, like any other form of physical activity, it will accept longer and more evolved motion. Try to increase the scope of complexity and the span of time in motion if you can.

🎯 Driving It Home

Beginning the process of getting your body in motion will help propel you into more involved action and movement as it retrains both your body and your brain. When you started reading this book, you probably did so with the idea that nothing was going to change in your life and that the life thief would continue to run your world. Instead, you are arming your world with an actionable plan to become a more productive and happier person. It is always good to have the right information, but that information will remain unusable until you turn it into action. In everything we do, it is the little steps that help us get there. You are using this new tool to begin this part of your new life journey, but you will also use it for the rest of your life. It is just one more weapon to help you fight the life thief and take your life back.

YOUR DECLARATION IS: *My little-action moments will lead to the big-picture actions that can change my world.*

 **Onward**

I have been discussing the importance of having a support team to help you understand the information I am presenting and also to help you learn to implement that information in your life. In the next chapter, I will help you understand how to identify your treatment team and how to let them help you with this part of the program.

CHAPTER 15

Starting Your Treatment Plan: Identifying Your Team and Letting Them In

Break out of your lonely world, let others in, and create your route to a brilliant new life.

PROCESSES TO EMPLOY: Brutal Honesty, I Over E, Present/Understand/Fix, Slowing Down Life's Pace, Internal Focus, Fact-Finding, Intelligent Decision Making, Listening, Trust

IN CHAPTER 5, I BEGAN PRESENTING THE idea of getting help to make the changes that are essential to relieving your depression symptoms. Whether it is a physician to help you with the physical and medicinal parts of your program or a professional counselor to provide you with someone to help you understand what is happening to you and to guide you as your treatment program unfolds, it is critical to have a network of professionals and support people in your corner. In Chapter 1, I began discussing how neurotransmitter imbalance can significantly affect your ability to understand and follow through with the changes that can help you work through your depression.

In those early chapters, I presented information about the symptoms of depression and acknowledged how difficult it can be for you to perform even the simplest of tasks. With your information-gathering skills minimized, the duration of your short-term memory impaired, and your motivation to follow through on what needs to be addressed in your life reduced, movement through the program seem like a monumental task. A support network is an integral part of the program, and without it, you remain alone, trying to make all these changes by yourself. That strategy has not worked to this point, and it will not work now.

YOUR NETWORK

Let's take a look at the people who need to be part of your support team. In Chapter 10, I began helping you put together a list of professionals and support people who could be part of your network. Your network is your support team, and you will use them to address your symptoms and difficulties, to varying extents, throughout the course of your treatment. Their levels of expertise will vary; some will provide you with professional expertise in a variety of areas, and others will be there to support you emotionally, and to help you address some of the day by day parts of the program. These may include helping you make small changes at home, assisting you with scheduling and advice from professionals, and being available to you in emergency situations.

Let's break your network into two complementary but distinctly different groups of individuals. First, there are your support people. These might include your advocate, family, friends, and anyone you feel can be there to hold you accountable and to support you emotionally and practically as you move through the processes of the program. Of even more importance are your network of professionals, each charged with the responsibility of addressing some specific issue related to your depression. In this chapter, I will expand on that list of support people and professionals I discussed in Chapter 10. It is important to know how to bring these professionals into your program and what to do with them when you do.

Your Support Network

Your Advocate

I have discussed the role your advocate plays in your program. Think of your advocate as a sponsor in a 12-step program. A 12-step sponsor understands all the various dynamics of addiction, has experienced the effects addiction has had in their own life, understands the program other members will be working with, will hold them accountable, and are there for their sponsee as needed. That said, your advocate does not have to be a person who has experienced acute depression. They do, however, need to understand its basic tenants, take it at face value, and validate what you are expressing to them. They need to be made aware of every part of your program and their role in it. They should never enable you to make the wrong choices or make excuses for you. They should, in step-by-step fashion, keep you focused on what you need to do and be there help you make the necessary decisions and take action when necessary.

Family and Close Friends

Family and friends are important since they provide a social component or, at the very least, a break from the loneliness that tends to characterize depression. Family and friends can also assume a watchdog role for you. There are times you may slip a bit or you may need both support and professional services, and they may see this before you do. Lastly, they can provide that emotional push, the love that is so important to help you through the desperate and troubled times depression can create. You might also include member of the clergy as part of your support team.

The Professionals

Professionals are a crucial part of your program since they specialize in areas that will be essential to your recovery. Here, I will expand upon the role of the professionals I initially introduced in Chapter

5 in your treatment plan. It is important to understand that, since depression is a multi-symptom disorder, engaging the help of professionals who specialize in treating the different symptoms and their causes are so advantageous.

A Primary Care Physician

Anytime you attempt to treat a physical problem that may have multiple symptoms, it is wise to have someone to coordinate communication between the various specialists. Your primary care physician will lay the foundation for everything that will take place in their office and in the offices of the specialists. They will do your wellness examination, make arrangements for your blood analysis, and gather all the information necessary to determine if you need help from other specialists.

Your primary care physician may also prescribe antidepressants and/or anti-anxiety medications to help you initially address the physical symptoms, if necessary. It is prudent to schedule visits with this person to monitor your medications and to review reports from other specialists at least twice a year. Keep your primary care physician aware of any concerns that arise throughout the course of your treatment.

A Psychologist or Professional Counselor

In Chapter 13, I touched on how important it is to retrain your brain. Having a professional with expertise in the dynamics and treatment of depression is essential to helping you understand what is happening in your life and to help you implement program(s) to address your depression. This professional may be a referral from your primary car physician, you may have heard about this person from other people, or they may be someone you found through your own research.

You will start with an introductory consultation, where your provider will gather all the information relevant to your case. The next few visits will continue the information-gathering process, but the initial parts of your treatment plan will also be presented to you.

Each week, you will discuss the components of your program, any and all information about past traumas, your feelings about yourself and those close to you, and important events in your life. The goal with this individual is to have a safe place to talk routinely. It helps curb the rumination process and helps you work through issues you may have been accustomed to keeping to yourself. This professional will also help you devise and alter your treatment plan as needed.

A Psychiatrist to Prescribe and Monitor Medication, if Necessary

For many people with depression, prescription medicines may be part of the program. Some of those medicines may be prescribed by a family physician, but in more severe cases, a psychiatrist may be involved to prescribe, mix, and monitor the medications. These are people with advanced degrees in psychology and medicine, so they understand the components of the depression and the medicines that will help you to address your neurotransmitter imbalance. You may see this person once a week for a month or so, and then, as long as another counselor is in working with you, they will be available to monitor your medication on a schedule that meets your treatment needs.

An Endocrinologist for Potential Thyroid Issues

An endocrinologist is one of the treatment specialists I mentioned in Chapter 7. An endocrinologist may not be part of your treatment team, but if your blood analysis indicates that there are past or present problems with your thyroid gland, such as if you have had all or part of your thyroid removed or have thyroid disease, this person may be part of your team. As I mentioned previously, your thyroid plays this significant role in hormone production, and in some cases, your depression may be caused or exacerbated by a thyroid that is not operating properly. An initial consultation with an endocrinologist would include discussing your thyroid numbers, and, if necessary, prescribing medications that address a hypothyroid or hyperthyroid issue.

An endocrinologist also specializes in hormone production and hormone abnormalities. So, while this person is treating your thyroid, if necessary, they are also able to do the testing to determine if any other hormonal issues may be contributing to your depression.

A Gastroenterologist for Gut Health

In Chapter 7, I briefly discussed how important gut health is to physical health and how problems therein can affect your body. Sometimes, it is the depression that causes gut issues, and sometimes the gut issues create an unhealthy environment that can either cause or exacerbate depression symptoms. The signs of poor gut health include autoimmune problems, such as thyroid issues; rheumatoid arthritis and Type 1 diabetes; digestive issues, such as irritable bowel syndrome; constipation; diarrhea; heartburn or bloating; sleep issues; skin rashes and allergies; sugar cravings; and unexplained fatigue or sluggishness. A gastrointestinal specialist will do the testing to determine whether the enzymes in your gut are healthy, and if they are not, there are various dietary changes and probiotics can be included in your program to correct the problem. positive movement forward.

A Gynecologist for Hormone-Related Issues

For women, the menstrual cycle plays a huge role in the way they feel physically, emotionally, and even intellectually. When gynecologists are addressing hormonal issues related to women's cycles, they may include an endocrinologist in the plan, or they themselves may do the testing. If there is a problem with your hormones, they may choose to treat those problems medicinally, or they may refer you to a specialist to help you. Sometimes, small doses of antidepressants are prescribed to help women deal with mood fluctuations related to menstruation or ovulation.

For women suffering from depression, I strongly advise discussing your problems with your gynecologist. If you do not have one or if you are not sure who to go to, most referrals to gynecologists come from other women. So, talk to your friends or family members about this. You can also obtain your referral from your family physician. It is important to keep in mind that depression has a high correlation to hormonal imbalance. Blood analysis can help, and regardless of whether you have depression or not, it is a good idea for women to have this specialist as part of their routine wellness program.

An Alternative Medicine Professional

Some people prefer to think outside the box of traditional medicine and incorporate the skills of alternative medicine practitioners in their plan. Traditional medicinal practitioners tend to have concerns about whether these individuals can treat acute and chronic cases of depression. However, you may find that alternative medicines are just what you need to start feeling better; nevertheless, be sure that the practitioner is properly educated in this discipline and is certified to provide patients with alternative medication. They should also possess training and experience treating depression, especially the more severe cases. Alternative practitioners can help you keep your body healthy, and, as I first said in Chapter 3, that may have a profound effect on your ability to combat your depression. Do, however, keep in mind, that since depression is primarily linked to neurotransmitter imbalance, whatever and alternative practitioner is doing, it must address that so important component of your depression.

Every good treatment plan can benefit from the inclusion of a good professional treatment team. These are the people who will help you diagnose your problem, provide you with the treatment that you need to address it, and be with you for as long as you need them to help you maintain your program. Your support people, those individuals who are not professionals but are informed enough and committed enough to be there for you, are so beneficial because they help remove the aloneness from your world. Depression can be a complex disorder. Be willing to take the time to identify these individuals and reduce the life thief's impact on your life. You deserve nothing less.

 **TIME TO TAKE ACTION**

1. Start the process of building a support and professional network with your advocate. There are many components to be addressed, and it makes good sense to have the support of these people.

2. Schedule that appointment with your primary care physician. This is the first step to help you get your treatment ball rolling. Don't forget to have a list of symptom you are experiencing. Discuss when the symptoms occur, how long they last, what impact they have on you, and anything else, whether you think it is important or not. Even the smallest detail can have a significant impact on your treatment program.

3. With your advocate, identify your support network, those family and friends who can be there for you as program reinforcements and to offer you emotional and practical support. Try to stay away from anyone who was overly emotional, or who you may have problems with.

4. Ask your advocate to attend your appointment with your primary care physician. This person should also attend any follow-up visits with your primary care physician and other practitioners.

5. If you are prescribed medication, your support network can help you pick up the prescriptions, and if necessary, help you to stay on schedule taking those medications. They may be essential to the plan.

6. Try to schedule regular time with your support network. Keep them close and informed. Discuss what is working, what may not be working, and how they can provide emotional support to reinforce what your professional treatment team is prescribing. They should not give you advice. Their only responsibility is to support you with the program your professionals are providing.

7. Do not procrastinate in getting the program started. Stay committed and consistent doing what the professionals in your network are advising. They cannot help you if you are unwilling to follow through. If you are having problems with any part of the program, don't keep it to yourself. Discuss it with your advocate, and definitely with your counselor and primary care physician.

 DRIVING IT HOME

Anything can be accomplished with a good plan to make it happen. Very rarely is a good plan, especially one that has as many moving parts as the treatment of depression, formulated and carried out by one individual. By utilizing your support network and those professionals who understand depression and can provide the necessary aspects of the treatment plan, you are stepping out of depression's aloneness and joining forces with a network that will begin the process of removing the life thief from your world.

YOUR DECLARATION IS: *I am no longer alone. My support network makes me strong, and I will work with them to defeat my depression.*

ONWARD

I have discussed the possibility of including medication in your treatment plan. In the next chapter, I will review this controversial treatment point, dispel some of the myths about these drugs, and give you enough information for you to decide, along with your physician and counselor, if it makes sense to incorporate them into your treatment plan.

CHAPTER 16

To Medicate or Not to Medicate: Taking the Emotion out of an Important Decision

Examine all your alternatives, but have a clear understanding of the information associated with all of them.

> **PROCESSES TO EMPLOY:** Brutal Honesty, I Over E, Present/Understand/Fix, Slowing Down Life's Pace, Internal Focus, Fact-Finding, Intelligent Decision Making, Keeping Life Simple

FOR MANY PEOPLE, ANTIDEPRESSANT MEDICATIONS WILL BE an important part of their depression treatment plan. This does not mean that you *must* include them to move forward. For some, however, the neurochemical imbalance is so pronounced that it needs to be addressed medicinally before moving on to other components of the plan. It is so important to take care of the physical part of the problem first, and for some people, medicine is the initial step that you need to take. Try not to overreact to what you read here. I am providing this chapter simply to help you understand the information so you can be more prepared when you talk to either your primary care physician or your psychiatrist (if one becomes part of your network).

In Chapter 2, I began to discuss neurotransmitters and how they affect the communication between the cells of your brain. Most antidepressants help relieve depression by improving the way these chemical messengers work, as they aid in communication between brain cells. Each type of antidepressant is designed to affect your body's neurotransmitters in slightly different ways.

Antidepressants have become a popular treatment choice for depression. Although antidepressants may not cure depression, they can reduce some of the symptoms. Not everyone needs to include antidepressants in their depression treatment program; for some, they are not necessary. On the other hand, especially in cases where the depression is more severe, it may be a good idea to at least explore the option. As I began to discuss in Chapter 1, sometimes medications could be a lifetime enterprise, or it may simply be included to help "jump start" your treatment plan.

For some people, a neurotransmitter imbalance can be a lifetime ordeal, so medication may be necessary to keep the body in a chemically balanced state. For other people, when antidepressants are prescribed and taken for a period of time, usually one to two years, the dose of the may either be reduced or the medication may be discontinued altogether. That usually has to do with the efficacy of the drug, whether or not it is still a requirement to address the physical needs, and if there may be any toxic effects developing. These are individual circumstances, and as I mentioned as we started to look at the personalization of your depression in Chapter 9, the possibility of you needing medication and for how long all depends on your personal life thief. You may need it—or not. You may need it for a longer period of time—or not. And you may only need it for a short period to prepare your body for the adjustments that are needed to continue on with your recovery program.

MAKING THE DECISION

The first and most important question is, how do you know whether you should try medication for depression? Here's what you need to ask yourself:

1. Have my symptoms been ongoing for at least a year, with little or no improvement realized?

2. Have I tried other approaches like counseling, and were they unsuccessful because I could not follow through with the plan?

If you have been suffering from symptoms of depression for a year or more and you have tried everything you can to relieve the pain, it might be prudent to at least discuss possibility of including prescription antidepressant into your treatment plan with your doctor. In the first nine chapters, I routinely discussed the notion of being informed and making intelligent decisions. Medicine is one of those areas where people react emotionally and often without the necessary information. Your first step is to learn as much as you can about antidepressants, and then discuss the possibility of including them in your treatment plan—or not.

The time may come when your physician suggests that you take medicine. This often occurs when your blood analysis either indicates a possible concern with one of your neurotransmitter-related levels, your thyroid, or some other contributing factor. Your doctor may have suggested other approaches like diet and exercise improvements, and perhaps you either could not follow through with the plans or they did not work. At that point, with other alternatives exhausted, medication may be suggested to initiate the process of symptom reduction.

In Chapter 4, we begin to discuss how depression needs to be treated as a physical condition first. Depression does affect your emotions and your intellect, but it is so important to improve your health and have your body healthy enough to fend off the attacks from the life thief. Antidepressants, then, might be an efficient way to get things started. Again, it's important to use them as a last resort, or in cases where the depression is so severe that you are unable to cope with it, or where it may lead to life threatening situations.

Very rarely do I find people who are overjoyed with the prospect of taking pharmaceuticals. Some see it as a weakness, some do not want to depend on an artificial substance, some are concerned about the side effects, and some simply do not like the idea of taking pills. Regardless of how you feel about medications, if nothing else has worked, it may be worth considering. There is some middle ground if you are wrestling with the idea of taking medication.

If you are still struggling with your depression and have tried other alternatives, it might make sense to do a trial run. This is where you take the medication for about three months. Most medicines take two to four weeks to reach a clinical level. This is where the medication has uploaded sufficiently and works at its optimal efficiency.

Doing an initial test allows you see how efficient the drug may or may not be for you, to experience any possible side effects, and possibly to experience some decrease in depressive symptomology. The advantage of doing a trial run is that no one says you have to stay on the medicine. You are not doing it for a year or two or for the rest of your life. You are simply taking an antidepressant for a brief time to see if it has a positive impact on your life. If you do not like it, you may discontinue it at any time under the guidance of your prescribing physician. This gives you a bit more control at a time where you may be feeling coerced to doing something you do not want to do.

WHAT'S RIGHT FOR YOU?

There are many types of antidepressants available that work in slightly different ways and have different side effects. Upon completion of your examination and blood analysis, you and your physician may decide to try the medication. Your primary care physician may prescribe the medications, or you may be referred to a psychiatrist, depending on what can work best for you. A nurse practitioner or physician's assistant may sit down with you and suggest which medication will work best for you. Make sure that they are acting on behalf of your doctor and that your physician is the one suggesting which medication to take. <u>Don't forget to suggest genetic screening</u>

first. This can provide the necessary information to help you determine which medicine is right for you. When seeking an antidepressant that is likely to work well for you, your physician should consider:

- **YOUR PHYSICAL HISTORY**—This includes any past illnesses or ongoing physical concerns, any other medicines you are taking, and any important conditions in your life.

- **POSSIBLE SIDE EFFECTS**—Side effects of antidepressants vary from one medicine to another and from person to person. Bothersome side effects such as dry mouth, nausea, weight gain, or sexual side effects like decreased libido can make it difficult to stick with treatment. Discuss possible major side effects with the prescribing physician or pharmacist. I will provide a list of the side effects of these medications shortly.

- **PERSONAL MEDICAL HISTORY**—Your physician should also consider your personal depression symptoms. Symptoms of depression can vary, and one antidepressant may relieve certain symptoms better than another. For example, if you have trouble sleeping, an antidepressant that causes some people to be calm or drowsy may be a good option. Also, if an antidepressant has been effective for your depression in the past, it may work well again.

- **FAMILY MEDICAL HISTORY**—How a medication worked for a blood relative, such as a parent or sibling, can indicate how well it might work for you. Remember, genetics do apply here. Also, at times, it may be important to consider medical conditions that other family members have experienced. This doesn't mean that you will have or experience those conditions, it's just good to know that they exist.

- **PREGNANCY OR BREASTFEEDING**—Certain antidepressants, such as Paxil, are discouraged during pregnancy. Pregnant women should be particularly cautious about antidepressants, and these should be discussed at length with your physician. You may want to get your gynecologist involved in the conversation.

- **OTHER HEALTH CONDITIONS**—Some antidepressants may cause problems if you have certain mental or physical health conditions. On the other hand, certain antidepressants may help treat other physical or mental health conditions along with depression. For example, many antidepressants may relieve symptoms of anxiety disorders or muscle pain. If you have other symptoms or physical concerns, make sure your physician knows this, since this this may indicate what medicine should be prescribed for you.

- **COST AND HEALTH INSURANCE COVERAGE**—Some antidepressants can be expensive, so ask if there is a generic version available and discuss its effectiveness. Also find out whether your health insurance covers antidepressants and if there are any limitations regarding which ones are covered and for how long.

Types of Antidepressants

Many types of antidepressants are available to treat depression. Let's take a look at the list of these medication groups.

- Selective serotonin reuptake inhibitors (SSRIs)—Physicians often start by prescribing an SSRI. These antidepressants generally cause fewer bothersome side effects and are less likely to cause problems at higher therapeutic doses than other types of antidepressants. SSRIs include fluoxetine (PROZAC), paroxetine (PAXIL, PEXEVA), sertraline (ZOLOFT), citalopram (CELEXA), and escitalopram (LEXAPRO).

- Serotonin and norepinephrine reuptake inhibitors (SNRIs)—Examples of SNRIs include duloxetine (CYMBALTA, DRIZALMA SPRINKLE), venlafaxine (EFFEXOR XR), desvenlafaxine (PRISTIQ), and levomilnacipran (FETZIMA).

- Atypical antidepressants—These antidepressants are called atypical because they do not fit neatly into any of the other antidepressant categories. More commonly prescribed antidepressants in this category include TRAZADONE, mirtazapine (Remeron), vortioxetine (TRINTELLIX), vilazodone (VIBRYD) and bupropion (FORVIVO XL, Wellbutrin SR, and others). Bupropion is one of the few antidepressants not frequently associated with sexual side effects.

- Tricyclic antidepressants—These antidepressants, such as imipramine, nortriptyline (Pamelor), amitriptyline, doxepin, and desipramine (NORPRAMIN) tend to cause more side effects than some of the newer antidepressants. So tricyclic antidepressants generally are not prescribed unless you have tried other antidepressants first without improvement.

- Monoamine oxidase inhibitors (MAOIs)—MAOIs such as tranylcypromine (PARNATE) phenelzine (NARDIL), and isocarboxazid (MARPLAN) may be prescribed, often when other medicines have not worked. This is because they can have serious side effects. Using an MAOI requires a strict diet because of dangerous (or even deadly) interactions with foods that contain tyramine (such as certain cheeses, pickles, and wines) and some medicines (including pain medicines, decongestants, and certain herbal supplements). Selegiline (EMSAM), an MAOI that you stick on your skin as a patch, may cause fewer side effects than other MAOIs. These medicines cannot be combined with SSRI's or other medicines that increase serotonin. Their coadministration can lead to increased serotonin levels, which could cause serotonin syndrome (Sjogren's (SHOW-grins) syndrome)—a rare but dangerous clinical condition. With this disorder, the body's immune system attacks its own healthy cells that produce saliva and tears. Sjögren's often occurs with other such disorders, such as rheumatoid arthritis and lupus. The main symptoms are dry mouth and dry eyes. Treatments include eye drops, medications, and eye surgery.

- Other medications—Your physician may recommend combining two antidepressants. Or they may add other medicines to improve antidepressant effects. This is called augmentation. Examples of antidepressant augmentation medicines include aripiprazole (ABILIFY), quetiapine (Seroquel), and lithium (LITHOBID).

- Medicinal marijuana—Today, people use marijuana for a variety of different ailments. Depression is one of those. People report improved depression symptoms as a result of regular marijuana usage. Keep in mind that marijuana is a central nervous system depressant, and though it may make you feel better now, there really is not enough research about how long-term use of marijuana impacts depression. Also, my experience is that people with depression who have used marijuana are more likely to become dependent on the drug. This is not to say that it cannot work for you, but I do caution you since we simply do not have enough research to make conclusive statements at this time. Be willing to talk about the possibility of marijuana usage with your physician.

The Side Effects

Some of the more common side effects associated with antidepressant medications are listed below. Most people taking these medications will experience a few of them, but others may have a more difficult time taking these medications. Not all medications will have serious side effects. However, it is a good idea to be aware of the potential side effects and to consult with your physician if you experience them. These side effects should improve within a few weeks, although some can occasionally persist. If they do not improve, or they worsen, or they cause you a level of discomfort that persists beyond a few weeks, consult your physician immediately. Remember, it's always a good idea to talk about the side effects when discussing the possibility of including medication in your treatment plan. Some of the side effects can include:

- Feeling agitated, shaky, or anxious
- Feeling possibly being sick
- Indigestion and stomachaches
- Diarrhea or constipation
- Loss of appetite

- Dizziness
- Not sleeping well (insomnia) or feeling very sleepy
- Headaches
- Loss of libido (reduced sex drive)
- Difficulties achieving orgasm during sex or masturbation
- Difficulties obtaining or maintaining an erection (erectile dysfunction)
- Dry mouth
- Slight blurring of vision
- Constipation
- Problems passing urine
- Drowsiness
- Dizziness
- Weight gain
- Excessive sweating (especially at night)
- Heart rhythm problems (arrhythmia), such as noticeable palpitations or a fast heartbeat (tachycardia)

Some people are particularly sensitive to medications, and the side effects for them may be worse than for others. Usually, your physician will prescribe one medication at a very low dose. This is how medication should be prescribed, since the goal is to take the smallest amount of medication to address your symptoms. If your physician feels you may need other medications, they may prescribe a second medicine to work with your initial prescription. At other times, your physician may prescribe one of the medications that acts as a booster to your initial prescription. When several prescriptions are part of the plan, it is always a good idea to see a psychiatrist. These practitioners are more skilled at mixing and matching antidepressant medications.

Antidepressants and the Risk of Suicide

In some cases, children, teenagers, and young adults under twenty-five may experience an increase in suicidal thoughts or behavior when taking antidepressants, especially in the first few weeks after starting or when the dose is changed. Most antidepressants are generally safe, but the U.S. Food and Drug Administration (FDA) requires that all antidepressants carry black box warnings—the strictest warnings for prescriptions. Regardless of your age, anyone taking an antidepressant should be watched closely for worsening depression or unusual behavior. If you begin to experience suicidal thoughts when taking an antidepressant, immediately contact your advocate, someone in your network, or your physician or psychiatrist. If none of these people are available dial 911 for emergency assistance. *This is a symptom you want to respond to immediately.*

INFORMED CHOICE

Just as not every person is created the same way, there is no one-size-fits-all program to treat depression. Some people will never need or be able to use medication, while for others, it can be a life saver. For those in between these two medicinal bookends, medication can, even for a short period of time, help set the stage for the changes you need to make. Medication is not something I ever quickly advise for my clients. I prefer to treat them with counseling and other therapeutic techniques first. There are times, however, when these approaches have been exhausted, but the suffering continues, or when the symptoms are so severe that they could instigate a crisis for client. At that time, I may quickly refer them to their primary care physician, or, at the very least, suggest at least a trial run on one medication.

As you move forward in your program, and as I have continued to advise, having the right information facilitates a good decision-making processes. Whether, or not, to take medication is a huge decision. All too often, people make appointments with physicians and have little to no information about any medications that may be prescribed. With the information presented in this chapter, you can be a bit more informed about what an antidepressant can do for you and whether you want to include one in your treatment plan. At the very least, you can ask intelligent questions about the medicines in question.

If you are still not sure about including an antidepressant in your treatment plan, consider the test I mentioned earlier in the chapter. Ask yourself two simple questions: have I exhausted all my options and if I have, does it make sense for me to pursue the possibility of including medicine as a test to see what happens. Whatever you do, discuss it with the people in your support network and get all the information you can from your physician. Your pharmacist is also a good the person to discuss antidepressant medicines with. Take your time as you gather the information about medicine, and ask all the questions you need to ask. Ask the doctors who are treating you to go slow so that you may understand everything what you are experiencing with the new medication. Try to keep your emotions in check and gather all the information you need before you make your decision.

TIME TO TAKE ACTION

1. Medications may or may not work for you. It is so important for you to get the information you need to make your decision. I presented some of it here. Enlist the help of your support network to help you get the information you need.

2. Your doctor can prescribe the medication for you, but before you take it, it also makes good sense to have a conversation with your pharmacist. Pharmacists are experts in medication. That is what their training is all about. Ask your pharmacist about the prescription medicines your physician is prescribing, and become a little bit more educated before you make your decision to put it in your body.

3. If you have exhausted your other options and your symptoms persist, you may want to consider a test run to determine if medications might be right for you. Talk that over with your physician.

4. If you do decide to take prescription medications, make sure you have a follow-up evaluative appointment scheduled with your physician no later than three weeks after the medication is prescribed.

5. If the side effects are overwhelming for you or new negative experiences appear, consult your physician immediately.

6. If you have decided to take prescription medications, stay away from other over-the-counter drugs, marijuana, and alcohol. If you choose to include these other drugs, they may interact with your prescription drugs. Ask your pharmacist if this could happen before you include over the counter medicines and other substances in your treatment plan.

7. If prescription medications do become part of your plan and your follow-up visit continues to provide positive information, make sure you schedule routine follow-ups every six months, just to make sure everything is going as planned.

 **DRIVING IT HOME**

The important takeaway from this chapter is that medicine may or may not be a viable option for you. Try not to make this an emotional decision. Heightened emotions seldom lead to good choices. Sound intellectual reasoning, valid information, and a good network of people to help you can make a world of informational difference. Armed with more information about medications and a network to help you make decisions, approach the subject of medication by asking the right questions, acquiring accurate information, and then discussing it with those professionals you are working with, and people close to you. Regardless of what decision you make, including a counseling component to help you with all your depression-related concerns is always strongly advised.

YOUR DECLARATION IS: *In everything I do, I will examine all the information, and I will make the decision that is right for me!*

 **ONWARD**

Throughout the chapters in this book, I have presented information that includes identifying and developing a network of support people and professionals to help you with your depression. In the next chapter, I will help you take a look at professional counseling and how to make that work for you, if this is something you are willing to do.

CHAPTER 17

The Safe Place: Bringing Your Person into Your Life

To connect with another human on the deepest levels can be an invaluable and immeasurable weapon in the fight against depression.

> **PROCESSES TO EMPLOY:** Brutal Honesty, I Over E, Present/Understand/Fix, Slowing Down Life's Pace, Internal Focus, Fact-Finding, Trust, Faith, Humility, Risk-Taking, Sustained Learning, Being Comfortable With Being Uncomfortable, Sustained Learning

AS FAR BACK AS CHAPTER 1, I suggested including a professional counselor in your fight to remove the life thief from your world. I discussed how lonely depression can make you feel and also that the battle you are attempting to wage against the thief is one you cannot fight alone. I have also discussed how depression robs you of your self-esteem and connects with the parts of your life that may include guilt, shame, and poor self-worth. All too often, people with depression feel unworthy of help and that no one really wants to listen to their problems.

The communication issues inherent in a life shrouded by depression are twofold:

1. People do not understand enough about depression and how it makes you feel. This can create a communication gap that makes you believe people are not interested.

2. Depression makes it difficult to communicate what you are feeling, since it robs you of your ability to accurately define your thoughts and emotions.

These two points suggest the need for someone who can understand you when you try to tell others how you feel and who will not judge or dismiss you. Your experience with a counselor, someone who has the expertise to help you define what you need to do to treat your depression can be life-changing. The time you spend with your counselor takes place in an environment that feels safe. That is so important for you. A counselor will design and implement a treatment program specifically tailored to you and will be willing, in step-by-step fashion, to support you as you begin to work with the new processes you are learning.

FINDING YOUR PERSON

We have discussed how depression makes even the easiest of tasks seemed like monumental enterprises. Deciding what to have for dinner or what to wear to the store can leave you feeling lost and directionless. More complex decisions concerning doctor's appointments, financial matters, relationship issues, and selecting a counselor with whom you will share your deepest and darkest secrets can seem to be insurmountable. There seems to be no logical information available to help you make these decisions, and even if there were, you probably would not trust the decision you are making.

By now, you understand that you cannot solve this depression thing on your own. You know that you are going to need help. Your advocate, as engaged as this person can be with regard to what you are experiencing, does not have the expertise to bring you through what you are experiencing. They can help you gather information and assist you in making some decisions, but they cannot and should not be asked to help you solve this problem. So, the next decision for you to make, with the help of your network, is who your personal counselor is going to be?

Matching the Need with the Resources

Your first order of business is to make a list of your needs. These are the problems that need to be solved. This will give you the information about what you need to change, what symptoms need to be addressed, and what the areas of expertise your prospective counselor should possess. Refer back to Chapter 3 to the list of depression types and their symptoms.

Your counselor should possess formal training in *psychology or counseling*. In some cases, you may want someone with a medical background, especially if medication is going to be in the picture. Of most importance is your prospective counselor's understanding of and expertise in treating various types of depression. This is where it gets a little sticky. Many therapists, though they may be professional counselors or even licensed psychologists, may not have an in-depth background in treating depression.

We have talked about depression as a physical, emotional, and intellectual condition, so the person who is going to counsel you should have an expertise in all those areas as they relate to depression. Anyone can talk to you about your problems, and they may even help you solve your everyday problems of living, such as relationships, past traumas, and work-related concerns, but depression on a level that drastically affects your life demands the attention of a professional with a solid background in treating depression—all aspects of it.

In some cases, you may be more comfortable with someone who is older and perhaps a bit more seasoned in their profession. In other cases, gender may be a concern for you. If you are part of the LBGTQ community, you may want someone who understands your life dynamics. The location of the counselor's office and whether insurance is accepted are also legitimate concerns. Though these are all important factors, the most important skill this professional needs to have is a thorough understanding of depression and the ability to treat *your* depression.

Today, many people receive counseling through online video platforms. Some conditions may be well suited for online counseling.

For the most part, however, depression tends to require a more in-depth approach. This does not mean online approaches cannot work. However, do keep in mind that if you receive counsel from your home, you are counselling from the very environment that you are depressed in. The person you are dealing with does not have the opportunity to see your body language and other important inflections that often provide information that is vital to the counseling situation. If you have no other option, it can certainly be advantageous for you, but do look for in-office counseling sessions at least part of the time.

As far as their qualifications are concerned, try to stay away from people who have coaching certificates and other short-term educational programs to attempt to treat your depression. Many life coaches do very good work, but depression is such an involved condition that you want to know the person counseling you has a strong enough background to understand neurology and basic anatomy. They should also have an in-depth knowledge of every component of depression. Remember, sometimes the symptomology between depression types can overlap. Your counselor should know where you are physically, emotionally, and intellectually, how the program is working for you at all times, and when and how to make changes, when necessary.

In Chapter 6, I began discussing the importance of your own personal network, those professional and support people who can help you attack the life thief. Another important question to ask your potential counselor is what kind of network they themselves use. They should be affiliated or at least have working relationship with a hospital, rehabilitation center, and other inpatient facilities, should those be needed. They should have arrangements with primary care physicians, a psychiatrist, and a pharmacist, if possible. These are the people I have advised you to include in your network. It certainly makes sense that your counseling professional would have them in theirs. At the very least, they need to be able to communicate with those people in your network.

The 7 Keys to Selecting Your Person

1. Make sure your counselor has an expertise in the dynamics and treatment of depression.

2. Match your counselor's abilities with your needs. Let your advodate or members of your support help you with this

3. If possible, try to see your counselor in their office. If this is not possible, make sure that they can treat your depression online. Make them commit to and explain how they will accomplish that.

4. Ask them if they are members of professional association like the American Psychological Association or the American Counseling Association. You may even be able to verify their credentials through these associations. A good source for qualified psychologists is on the Psychology Today website.

5. Ask your primary care physician and other members of your network if they know anything about the counselor you are considering. You may even include your primary care physician or other members of your network in your search process and in your decision regarding which counselor to choose.

6. Make sure your counselor has their own professional network in case you need referrals that are beyond the scope of their level of expertise.

7. Be willing to schedule a consultation with a counselor you are considering without the commitment of continuing the counseling immediately. If you feel comfortable with them, that is a good first step. Ask them how they plan to help you through your depression. Make sure you feel good about what you are experiencing in that first consultation.

Here is a short checklist of the questions you should ask a counselor during your first consultation.

- Can you show me your counseling credentials?
- Can you tell me about your expertise regarding the dynamics and treatment of depression?
- Do you have affiliations with other professionals in case I need services in different areas?
- Do you also specialize in family counseling, and can I bring members of my support team with me from time to time?
- Are you available for me in your office as well as in virtual counseling sessions?
- Are you available during off hours in case I need contact you during an emergency?
- Do you take my insurance (if you have insurance), or is there a sliding scale for payments?

Depression is one of those conditions that can keep you isolated and lost in a dark, motionless world. Having a network to help you through your treatment process is crucial, but just as crucial is the need for your own personal safe person. Including the services of a professional counselor can help you address symptoms related to your depression, but it also gives you your personal safe space with someone you can trust to help you approach those parts of your life that may be difficult to discuss with others. Step out of the darkness and let someone else be part of your life. Begin the process of trusting another human being so you may shed light in what has been a dark place to live.

TIME TO TAKE ACTION

1. Having your own safe person to talk to is a crucial step away from the life thief. Be willing to take this step.

2. Invite your advocate to help you find someone you can be comfortable enough to open up to. Refer back to the 7 Keys to Selecting Your Person in this chapter to help you with the process.

3. Make an initial appointment for a consultation with the person you select.

4. If possible, take your advocate or someone you trust to the first session. They will help you provide more background and details about your concerns to yor counselor.

5. Ask the questions I listed earlier during your initial consultation. Make sure their answers provide you with enough information to ensure they have the ability to help you.

6. If all goes well in the first session, make an appointment for the second session that day. The first two sessions are crucial in getting the process started.

7. Journal about your counseling sessions. This gives you the opportunity to review what happened in your most recent session and can also set the stage for what needs to occur in your next session.

 **DRIVING IT HOME**

When you are setting up your network to help you through your depression, never forget that this is your life you are talking about. Including a professional counselor who is always going to be there for you, understands what you are thinking and feeling, and knows how to take you through the treatment and eventually recovery process from depression is essential. You have the right to obtain the absolute best care available. Accept nothing less, be warm and respectful, but let your person know that this is what you expect from them. Depression can make you feel ugly and broken. You are not. You are beautiful, and it's time to feel good about yourself.

YOUR DECLARATION IS: *I will let someone in to help me. I will not do this alone anymore.*

 **ONWARD**

Now that you are securing the services of a counselor to help you face past, present, and future challenges to become that whole person you want to be, it is time to learn how to introduce change into your life. In the next chapter, we will look at how change can help you become the healthy person you want to be, one step at a time.

CHAPTER 18

Accepting Change: Out of the Darkness, One Little Step at a Time

Change is not a monster, and it will not kill you. Learn how to incorporate this life saving strategy in your antidepression game plan.

PROCESSES TO EMPLOY: Brutal Honesty, I Over E, Present/Understand/Fix, Slowing Down Life's Pace, Internal Focus, Fact-Finding, Risk-Taking, Trust, Being Comfortable With Being Uncomfortable, Sustained Learning, Time/Energy Management, Incremental Forward Movement

WITH THE SUPPORT FROM YOUR NETWORK, and with the help of your counselor, you are now ready to increase the scope of your program. This is where you begin to make those small changes that help you set the course for the rest of your life. When you were alone with no one to turn to, no one who understood you, and with no forward vision about how to change your life, you were at the mercy of the life thief. Your willingness to make the initial decision to get better and then to follow that resolution by identifying and including a support network into your plan got things started. Now, it is time for you, along with guidance from your counselor, to begin to make those life changes.

By reviewing your list of symptoms that are plaguing you and having an idea of what needs to change in your life, you can begin to step out of that dark demonic world and do things a little differently. This means you are going to make changes in your life. The initial thought that things can be better is both appealing and nerve wracking. You have tried to make changes in the past, and nothing seemed to work. It's hard to trust the notion that things might finally improve. However, remember you were trying to do this on your own. Now you have professionals, support people, and a new direction in your life. Now it is time for change.

UNCHARTED TERRITORY

I have discussed how your mind adapts to what you are presenting it with and what you experience in your life. For as long as you have had depression, your mind has had to adapt to neurotransmitter imbalance, loneliness, isolation, and feelings of guilt and shame, to mention just few. Your brain has been tasked with the responsibility to help you survive in a directionless and unmotivated way of living. As it adjusted to the thief's unrelenting attacks, however, it kept you locked in an aimless and painful world, destined to relive one lifeless day after another. This is the time you have been waiting for. The cavalry has arrived, and the possibility of being rescued from this drab and listless world is right in front of you. The territory ahead, however, is new. You have never experienced it before. You may not be sure who lives out there. You know you do not want to stay in the world you have been living in any longer, and you know you want to make the changes necessary to feel better. What is unclear is what those changes are and how you are going to feel when you get there.

The first and most important way of looking at this new change is that everyone who goes through what you are going through experiences this. Many people have navigated through the insecurities that change introduces in their lives, becoming happier and healthier people. You can through this, too. You will be making changes, and you will be asked to take some risks. Try not to become overwhelmed by the thought of change. Keep in mind that you are not alone and that change will be introduced at a pace you can understand and implement, under the guidance of your counselor and with the assistance of your support network.

There are two kinds of change people can experience throughout their lives. The first are changes we, ourselves, introduce into our lives. We do this because we believe that something cannot remain as it has been or because the conditions of our lives have altered and we may need to to accommodate those shifts. The other type of change is one of which we are not always initiating. As I have said previously, life is a dynamic enterprise; it never stops evolving. Our world does not stay the same, and each adjustment presents us with new challenges and new demands. You know how hard it has been to deal with even the simplest aspects of your life under the heel of depression. Now, you are going to be asked to make some changes. Do not worry; there is a simple, straightforward way to make this happen, and you can do this.

SLOW AND STEADY

I have frequently reiterated that no change occurs quickly. In fact, the best changes you will ever make in your life will occur slowly, in step-by-step fashion. Growth and your ability to understand and implement change occurs most efficiently when you go slow. Going slow allows you to carefully process what has to change, how it is going to change, and your part in that change while providing you with enough time to adjust if necessary and to ask questions along the way. Going slow also allows you to pause, when necessary, to take a breath, and to return to the changes you are making when you are ready. Nothing facilitates learning, that repetition overtime I mentioned earlier, than going slow

There is a critical point to consider here. During depression, while those basic tasks were so overwhelming, your brain got used to becoming overwhelmed and doing its best not to examine information for fear of what it may do to you, so either you could not start the process or you quit relatively soon after starting. This is depression's modus operandi—that is, the process the life thief uses to keep you down and out. As a result, you were often defeated before you started.

Your counselor, along with your support network, is going to help you change the way the life thief's process works. Your new process will be slowly introduced and made easy for you to understand, and it will help you make the changes you need to make without turning your life upside down and inside out in the process. This is the way the steps of change should look for you.

THE 8 STEPS OF CHANGE

1. After a discussion of your symptoms and/or areas of need with your counselor, you decide to make a small change.

2. You decide that the change will occur in small, incremental steps that are easy to understand and, with the assistance of your counselor and your support network, reasonable for you to do.

3. You, along with your counselor, will discuss the first step of the change until you understand it. You should be presented with exactly what you must do and exactly what your counselor and your support network will do to assist you with the steps of the change.

4. Based on the information that explained how the change will occur, you will attempt to implement that change into your life. If you are having difficulty, you will let your support network know, and they will take steps to assist you in the process.

5. You will discuss your progress and any concerns you have with your counselor in weekly counseling sessions and, if necessary, through telephone calls or other communication methods throughout the week.

6. Begin journaling about your progress with the small change(s) to help you see how well you are doing, how you are feeling about what you are doing, and what questions or concerns you may have.

7. You will focus only on the small change that is being discussed and not try to get ahead of yourself.

8. When you feel confident that you were able to make that small change, you will discuss the next change step in detail with your counselor until you understand it and are ready to implement steps necessary to facilitate this next change.

All this hinges on your willingness to accept the idea of making changes in your life, your dedication to the process of change, and your continued commitment to work with your counselor and support team to make every effort to address these simple changes. Everyone in your support network understands that change is difficult for you, that your chemical imbalance has caused you significant pain, and fear and what that imbalance has done to you thus far. While no one should take it easy on you or let you fail, they should be understanding of your experience. You want your support network to be firm and not enabling of wrong decisions or quitting, but empathetic enough to understand what you are feeling. Be open with them always.

FAILURE IS NOT AN OPTION

No one can discount the pain and suffering you have experienced at the hands of the life thief. Your supporting professionals and your support network understand this, but it is their job to help you through your negative feelings and into a more positive way of life. From time to time, then, you might feel as though they are pushing a bit hard. This is where you must try to assess whether it is really them pushing too hard or you resisting the push. Nothing about depression is easy, and there will be times when their efforts to move you forward are so exhausting that you may want to take shelter in your old, depressive ways, at least briefly, to get a reprieve and catch your breath. Keep in mind that those old depressive ways are where the life thief lives, and you want to avoid that at all costs.

There is nothing wrong with short pauses in the program. No one expects you to quickly jump into a new living format and be perfect there. From time to time, you will need a break. There is nothing wrong with that, but you must be upfront and honest with your network to handle that. Without trying to make things easy on yourself or remove yourself from the work, and with the input of your counselor, schedule short breaks into your treatment plan. No one can fault you for this; this is the way to live a healthy life. We work hard, we play hard, and we take breaks. However, we always return to the work in timely fashion, and with steadfast commitment to continue your forward movement.

If you are going to leave this life thief behind, it will take commitment, hard work, and the support of your network to get there. Negative thinking has no place here, and that old idea that this will never stop or that you will never get better has absolutely no place in your new life plan. Failure has absolutely no place in your new life. You are going to get a bit uncomfortable, but feeling discomfort because you are moving forward and growing is a small price to pay to rid yourself of the life thief's dark and painful presence. Keep focused, stay committed, trust your network, and know that if you stay with the program, good things are going to happen.

TIME TO TAKE ACTION

1. Be willing to take the small risks and accept the new changes in your life. Recognize that periods of discomfort are growth periods made up of little steps that will gradually provide the happy life you are looking for.

2. Make your counselor your best (growth) friend. Discuss everything with this person. Trust what they have to say and work diligently to achieve the small goals you are both defining.

3. Try not to get overwhelmed. Take small steps, each defined with an incremental approach that allows you to accomplish one small goal at a time.

4. Keep your advocate and your support network close. There may be times when you want to retreat, but never put distance between yourself and them.

5. Understand that change is a marvelous program gift. Use the 8 Steps of Change I presented in this chapter as a guide to keep you focused on the plan you have chosen to undertake.

6. Be focused and tenacious. Stay positive, and never consider the possibility of failure. With your counselor, routinely discuss each and every step of your plan and your feelings about what is changing.

7. Journal about your new changes. This helps you see what you are accomplishing, how you think and feel about what is happening, and what you may need to discuss further with your counselor and support network.

 **DRIVING IT HOME**

Change is not a monster, and it is nothing to fear. As you begin to implement your treatment plan, do expect some issues related to motivation, concentration, and commitment. Once again, no one expects you to do this all at once. The feeling that things need to be accomplished quickly is part of what made the problem worse for you. Focus on small changes—little, incremental, step-by-step modifications that will help you change the way you think and feel overall. Try to go into this part of the program with that in your mind. Trust your counselor and your support network. If you do, little by little, good things will happen.

YOUR DECLARATION IS: *I will make small, step-by-step changes, and they will change my life!*

 **ONWARD**

In Chapter 18, I mentioned how important it is stay focused and not give up. It is important to keep your eye on the prize, and in the next chapter, we will discuss how not giving up can help you understand just how powerful you can be.

CHAPTER 19

Learning How Powerful You Can Be: Embracing "I Can"

For those unwilling to surrender, all the wonders of the world are waiting to be embraced.

PROCESSES TO EMPLOY: Brutal Honesty, I Over E, Present/Understand/Fix, Slowing Down Life's Pace, Internal Focus, Fact-Finding, Trust, Faith, Humility, Sustained Learning, Commitment, Journey Living, Incremental Forward Movement

SOME OF THE MOST AMAZING ACCOMPLISHMENTS in human history were made by people who failed repeatedly, refused to give up, and eventually embraced the joy of a successful venture. If everyone could simply decide to do something and then quickly make it happen, we would all be filled with high self-esteem and tremendous self-confidence. The world, however, does not work quite that way. The typical formula requires having an idea, developing a plan, and then doing your best to make that plan work. Since it is impossible to plan for every pitfall and unexpected turn of events along the way, we can expect a reasonable number of unsuccessful attempts.

You do not need to have depression to be derailed by unforeseen events, planning that did not incorporate all the necessary information, and good old human error. Anyone can experience difficulty, failure, and motivation issues that can make sticking with a task seem like a monumental effort. Unsuccessful attempts to do something, in addition to falling short of your goal, can have two important positive defining benefits:

1. They provide more information about what needs to be done to correct what you did wrong in the initial attempts. This helps you refine your approach, increasing your potential for success in future attempts to reach your goal.

2. Each time you try something, are unsuccessful, and then try it again, you can become stronger and more confident, providing you are willing to continue. If you do, you will learn more about the process of not giving up.

This is precisely the philosophy you need to use as you continue your program. Your mind can be inundated with the intellectual and emotional fallout from failed past attempts as you attempted to rid yourself of depression. In the past, when you tried something and either lacked motivation to start or, after a few small steps, decided your present attempt was a failure, you quit and returned to the life thief's dismal prison. In short, and understandably so, quitting was always a possible part of your plan. That changes now.

ACCEPTING THE CHALLENGE

Let's take a look at some challenges that will come your way as you begin working with your counselor. I have discussed how changes will be presented in small, step-by-step increments, but more likely than not, you are not used to accepting and implementing these challenges. That is not something to be overly concerned about. This is where trusting your network, particularly your counselor and advocate, becomes so important. Everything you do will be a step-by-step process, and your counselor and support team will be with you every step of the way. I will provide you with a practical application for this process in Chapter 20.

If you were a stranger in a foreign land, you would not speak the language of that land or know all the little markers that you need to function there. If you were fortunate, you would find someone to guide you through all these little nuances. You would need to trust that person and take their advice to stay away from danger and enjoy yourself while you are there. The same dynamic applies as you explore the steps in your treatment plan through an unfamiliar world with professional and supportive guides to help you navigate through it.

The life thief had you convinced that you could accomplish very little in this world and almost nothing would ever change. Soon, you learned to believe that about yourself. Past failures, the inability to move forward, concentration and focus issues, and the firm belief that, regardless of what you tried, there was absolutely no way in the world to do it. This left you experiencing repeated failures that left you discouraged and wary of your own abilities. Now, you are not alone in this foreign land; you have people to interpret the language who are more understanding about how you feel and who will be there for you for the long run. It is time to accept the challenge, trust your network, and do not quit.

THE FORMULA FOR PROGRAM PERSISTENCE

Since you are removing the word "quit" from your program vernacular, I will replace it with a formula that can keep you locked in your program protocol and focused on the goals you need to achieve success. In Chapter 18, I presented you with the 8 Steps of Change. Using them, you have an applicable blueprint to understand the changes you are preparing to implement in your treatment program, and you have your counselor and support network to help you address them. To keep you focused, determined, and persistent so that you stay in the treatment game, here is the next little program gem.

The 10 Principles for Program Persistence

1. Use positive language, and nothing but positive language.

2. Keep your professional team and support network involved in everything you do, every day.

3. Approach every part of the plan and every little step you take with an attitude that says, "I will do what it takes to make it happen every day."

4. Let go of past trials and unsuccessful ventures. That is in the past. Try to learn from those attempts and focus all your efforts on what you are doing today.

5. Never skip a counseling session, and at the end of every session, make sure you know what you must do to help move your plan forward.

6. Each day, include little periods of action into what you are doing. It does not matter what you do; just keep your body moving.

7. Learn to say no to the life thief. You are working with small steps. Your depression will want you to check out and do nothing. Refuse the urge. Push yourself and get back to your plan.

8. If you are having trouble with your plan, contact your counselor or your advocate and get that little push you need to keep going.

9. Always think of yourself as capable and worthy of the time it takes to dispel the life thief from your life.

10. Have a plan for every day. Journal about what you have done and your plan for your next little step. Let everyone in your network know what you are doing. This helps to secure the success you are working toward.

Your personal life thief has always had the ability to lock you in your room with the lights out, the curtains drawn, and the world completely shut out. As your brain made the adjustment to this way of life, it became their routine way you lived. I began your lesson in depression with a deep dive into depression-related information. My goal was to give you the knowledge and understanding of the condition that was robbing you of your happiness, your productivity, and your world and everything in it.

We moved from that information to preparing you for the next step in the process, which was to set up your support network, you're professional/medical team, and finally you are a professional counselor. With these people in place and with your willingness to accept the responsibility of sticking with the program and never quitting, good things can happen. It will take some time, but if you don't get started, the only plan you will have is to remain where you are. Needless to say, that is unacceptable.

BECOMING YOUR OWN POWERFUL PERSON

Becoming a powerful person has less to do with conquering the life thief than it does with learning the process to do so. Many people focus their efforts on the grandiose end result they are dying to see happen. The only way to get to that end result is by developing your plan, sticking with it, and maintaining accountability and commitment to make it come to fruition. *Power is about acquiring the information you need about any given subject and learning how to turn that information into action without quitting.*

Power does not have to say, "I did it." It only has to say, "I know I can, and I will." It does not know negative self-language, and it does not understand how to quit. Power understands that there will be difficult times and little failures along the way. By staying consistent with the process and never quitting, power understands how to assert itself. It does not doubt itself, and it believes that no matter what comes along, it possesses the ability to create success.

So, be willing to accept the challenge. It doesn't matter if the work is hard, and it doesn't matter if it takes longer than you would like it to. The only thing that matters is that you stay in the game. Again, you are not the only player in the game anymore. You have a team of people who understand the dynamics of depression and how to help you defeat this unwanted life-stealing nemesis.

The truth of the matter is that regardless of what you elect to do, you are going to be uncomfortable. You can choose to be uncomfortable in the company of the life thief, drowning in darkness, or you can choose to be uncomfortable surrounded by people who love you, want to support you, and have the expertise to help you come through this. That choice is yours and yours alone. Be unwilling to quit. Be willing to stick with your treatment program and learn the process that can empower you. It's time to step out of the darkness and into a brilliant new light.

TIME TO TAKE ACTION

1. Make the decision to be a person who is unwilling to quit. Your persistence, along with all the support and expertise that are now in your corner, will create the powerful new you if you just stay with it.

2. Use the 10 Principles for Program Persistence every day. Tape them to your refrigerator or your bedpost if that helps. Just keep them available and always ready to use.

3. Stay close to your support network. When you experience even the slightest inclination to move backward, get these people involved. Get that gentle push you need to keep going.

4. If you are having a difficult time, journal about what you are thinking and feeling. Also write down why you think you are having the problem. Take this to your next counseling session and let your counselor work with you to move past your sticking spot.

5. Keep yourself in action, and when you feel as though that dark, dingy room with the curtains drawn is calling your name, tell it to go bother someone else. You are not interested. Then, involve your support network quickly.

6. Know that power comes from an unrelenting will that never quits. Get the information, formulate the plan, implement it, and never, ever back off.

 **DRIVING IT HOME**

A more powerful version of you is waiting. Keep in mind that how you wage war will define your power. A tenacious and unwavering battle will move you past those little failures and help you find your way into the success you are looking for. This is a war you are going to wage one battle at a time, one step at a time. You are not alone on the battlefield, and the people who are in your corner deeply care about you and are there to help you become successful and happy.

Never, ever quit. If you get discouraged, call in reinforcements. The biggest key is that when you need help, you must get it fast. Don't just think about getting help, and don't assume either people don't want to hear about it or may not want to be there for you. None of that is true. Do not procrastinate when it comes to getting help. Wage war. Never surrender. Keep your reinforcements close and introduce yourself to the powerful new you.

YOUR DECLARATION IS: *I will never quit. I am powerful!*

 **ONWARD**

I have been discussing your plan to move forward and how it will evolve through incremental small steps forward. In the next chapter, I will break this down even further and give you a functional, actionable way to understand and implement this life-saving procedure.

CHAPTER 20

Incremental and Consistent: The Step-by-Step Approach Explained

The most important movements in life are always small and consistent. Learn the importance of simple growth that never stops.

PROCESSES TO EMPLOY: Brutal Honesty, I Over E, Present/Understand/Fix, Slowing Down Life's Pace, Internal Focus, Fact-Finding, Incremental Forward Movement

IN CHAPTERS 18 AND 19, I EXPOUNDED on the process of slow, incremental steps forward. We have discussed how depression has a significant impact on your focus, concentration, motivation, and sound, logical decision-making. Your counselor is going to collect the important information about your life, as well as exploring how you think and feel with you. Then, they will design your treatment program. It will be up to you, along with help of your counselor and your support network, to implement that plan.

I have discussed the importance of knowledge in any undertaking, as well as how knowledge with a viable, step-by-step plan creates powerful movement forward. In this chapter, I am going to make the process of incremental forward movement a little easier to understand. I will break it down into basic, practical, easy-to-understand steps to help you move your program forward, and then I will break each step down to make them actionable for you.

> **THE 10 STEPS OF INCREMENTAL FORWARD MOVEMENT**
>
> 1. Define want you want to change.
> 2. Gather the facts you need about what you want to change.
> 3. Prioritize the information your counselor gathered to help you formulate your plan to address the change.
> 4. Break your facts down into the smaller, easier-to-implement components.
> 5. Organize the information into a step-by-step plan.
> 6. Routinely make time to assess the plan and your progress in it.
> 7. Execute your plan one step at a time.
> 8. Discuss your progress routinely with your counselor.
> 9. Make small changes to your plan, if necessary.
> 10. Discuss your progress and move to the next step in the change when you are ready.

Now, I am going to expand on each of these steps to provide you with a better understanding of how to implement them. Don't worry if it seems a bit complicated. These are steps you are going to take with your counselor. However, it's advantageous for you to begin to understand them to make the implementation of your program with your counselor more efficient.

1. **DEFINE WHAT YOU WANT TO CHANGE**—Defining your change is one of the most important first steps you will need to successfully implement your change. This does not require detailed analysis; you simply need to tell your counselor that something is holding

you back, causing you pain, and stopping you from living a happy, productive life. Just state the problem.

2. **GATHER THE FACTS YOU NEED ABOUT WHAT YOU WANT TO CHANGE**—To fully understand what you want to change, you need to discuss, in detail, what is bothering you, how it developed, and how it is making you think and feel. Your counselor may ask for a more detailed personal history to gain insight into how your problem developed. You should also discuss what is currently happening with that problem, along with a detailed synopsis of everything presently occurring in your life. Your counselor may have many questions during this step of the process. Remember, the more comprehensive and detailed information they have, the better equipped they are to help you deal with that problem. This information will give your counselor a better idea of how to help you move forward.

3. **PRIORITIZE THE INFORMATION YOUR COUNSELOR GATHERED TO HELP YOU FORMULATE YOUR PLAN TO ADDRESS THE CHANGE**—Very often, your information will suggest several steps that must be taken to help you with your problem. This is where you and your counselor will prioritize the information and decide which step should be addressed first. This makes it easier for you, because change always depends on how the information is presented and in what order it is addressed. This is partly why you may have had problems implementing your plan in the past. You simply did not know where to start. Now, with your counselors help, you will.

4. **BREAK YOUR FACTS DOWN INTO THE SMALLER, EASIER-TO-IMPLEMENT COMPONENTS**—Now that you know where to start, your counselor will help you break that part of the process down into easier, step-by-step components. Previously, you likely tried to implement an entire plan of change without an efficient starting spot and without breaking it down into smaller, more functional steps. Now, you have a starting spot, you have identified the first small step that needs to be taken, and with your

counselor's help, you will define how this the first step begins and progresses.

5. **ORGANIZE THE INFORMATION INTO A STEP-BY-STEP PLAN**—In a continuation of the previous step, your counselor will help you organize the information into easier steps. This step is important because everyone interprets information differently, and you are part of that everyone. Your counselor, having already prioritized your information, will help you organize it in a way that you can efficiently interpret it, and begin to execute it while discussing your progress and asking questions when necessary.

6. **MAKE TIME TO REASSESS AND ADJUST THE PLAN WHEN NECESSARY**—As I have consistently mentioned throughout discussion, there is no expectation that you quickly adjust to the changes I am suggesting here. They are going to be times when you have to pause, catch your breath, and refocus your attention. This will occur in two ways: First, pauses may be built into your plan at the time you and your counselor discuss what needs to change. Second, there may be times when you are confused or have trouble focusing on the plan, and you may just need a short break followed by an efficient reboot to get things going again. These pauses should always be short in duration, maybe a few hours or a day, and should always be something you communicate to your counselor before pausing your program. There should also be agreed upon return time to your plan.

7. **EXECUTE YOUR PLAN ONE STEP AT A TIME**—In this step, you will execute the first step of the plan exactly as you and your counselor discussed it. Your counselor will give you the little nudge you need to get things started, and the plan may even begin in your counselor's office. You should have the option of staying in touch with your counselor as you are attempting to make the changes.

8. **DISCUSS YOUR PROGRESS ROUTINELY WITH YOUR COUNSELOR**—Implementation and communication go hand in hand

when it comes to change. This means that you are constantly communicating with your support network and your counselor about the progress you are making and any problems you are having. This is also where your network, without enabling you, may gently push you to hold you accountable. This is a no-nonsense part of the plan. You are implementing your plan for change in a step-by-step fashion that has been made simple to implement. It is up to you to also hold yourself accountable and to get things done.

9. **MAKE SMALL CHANGES TO YOUR PLAN, IF NECESSARY**—In step 6, I discussed the little pauses and possible changes that may be necessary to the success of your plan. This is crucial. The plan never changes because you are unwilling to work with it or have decided to refocus on negativity and stagnation. If you continue to revert to the life thief's way of doing things, you will remain attached to it. These pauses give you a short break from the plan, but returning with the understanding that the work must continue is paramount to your success. When you discuss any difficulty you are having, your counselor and support network will help you fine-tune your plan, but they need to get you right back on track. This is exactly what you need at this time. There is no letting up now.

10. **DISCUSS YOUR PROGRESS, AND MOVE ON TO THE NEXT STEP IN THE CHANGE WHEN YOU ARE READY**—Your counselor will discuss everything you are doing, and how long it should take to accomplish the various steps in your plan. Your network will always be there to help you along the way, and at the end of that time, you will need to be ready to begin the next incremental little step. The preparation for this next step will not take as long as it did when you started the first prioritized step. Your counselor already has the information necessary to help you with the changes you need. Remember, steps were discussed and prioritized. You are simply going to the next prioritized item and beginning the process to address the next little step.

YOUR POWERFUL INFORMATION ORGANIZER AND PLAN IMPLEMENTER

Your brain is a natural information organizer. It operates best when you provide it with *information connectors*. These are smaller pieces of information that connect well to each other, allowing the brain to develop a coherent intellectual-processing picture for you to work with. For example, if your plan is to challenge yourself to take a walk around the block, just leaving the house and attempting to make the trip could be a daunting venture. Breaking it down into smaller steps, like what time you will be leaving the house, what you are going to wear, the route you will take, and how much time you are going to spend on your walk, breaks a larger, more complicated experience into smaller, easier-to-digest components. These are your information connectors. Going slow with smaller, incremental pieces of information allows a plan to evolve at a pace that is more consistent with your brain's natural design.

To give you another way to look at information connectors, consider what happens to you when you are watching a movie or a television show where the writer does not provide the information connectors to bring you from one point in the plot to another. When this happens, you find yourself saying, "How did they get there?" However, if the information connectors are efficiently built into the script, you can follow the storyline, and the film makes more sense to you. This is what little steps are. They are information connectors that help you understand all the little components of the plan and how they can evolve, as well as your part in executing those steps.

All too often, the way we force our brain to operate runs counter to the way it is designed to run. One of the reasons people overreact to forward movement is that they tend to focus their energies on the desired outcome. When this happens, the ground to be covered between the plan's starting point and the finish line appears undefined and enormous. The task is simply too large for the brain to comprehend. It is also missing some of the information necessary to move forward, information that can be more efficiently addressed using a step-by-step blueprint.

Your brain is a powerful information organizer and plan implementer. The neurotransmitter imbalance that has affected it changed the way it was intended to operate and left you unable to understand how to process information and to use all those little connectors, those little steps that help you accomplish things you would like to do. As I have said repeatedly, nothing about depression is easy, but with your network to support you, professionals to help you diagnose and make changes where necessary, and a personal counselor to guide you through the process, that powerful organizer has what it needs to become a magnificent plan implementer.

 TIME TO TAKE ACTION

1. Renew your commitment to use your support network and team of professionals to help you diagnose your problem(s), gather information, and implement your plan.

2. Use 10 Steps of Incremental Forward Movement. Discuss them with your counselor. They are an invaluable tool to help you break down information and design and implement the plan to change your life.

3. Make sure your support network understands how you are making your changes. Keep them aware of every step you take and of how they can assist you in the process.

4. Journal about the changes you are making. Include what you are doing in every step, how you feel about it, and any difficult experiences you are having. Also, don't hesitate to give yourself a pat on your back as you journal. What you're doing is hard work, and you deserve credit and praise for it.

 **DRIVING IT HOME**

Up to now, you have done everything you could to remove the life thief from your world. Now, you understand how a viable approach along with guidance and support can take you through this process. The 10 Steps of Incremental Forward Movement can help you understand not only what to implement but also how to make your plans become your reality. There is work ahead of you, but there is also a wonderful and efficient process at your fingertips, along with all the support and encouragement you need to make this happen. Your life does not belong to the depression demon. It is *your* life. It is time for you to take control of it.

YOUR DECLARATION IS: *One small step at a time, I am going to change my world!*

 **ONWARD**

Now that you have your counselor and your support network assisting you into your movement forward, it is important to understand not only how to make changes but also how to apply them in your life. In the next chapter, I am going to further show you how to incorporate the changes you are making into your life in an incremental fashion. I included this chapter to reinforce what I taught you in chapter 19. At times, it may seem repetitive, but it is so important to understand how to apply what you are learning.

CHAPTER 21

Learning to Live in Your New World: Applying Your Changes One Step at a Time

It's everything you've always wanted. Be willing to take the time to learn how to live in your new world.

PROCESSES TO EMPLOY: Brutal Honesty, I Over E, Present/Understand/Fix, Slowing Down Life's Pace, Internal Focus, Fact-Finding

YOU HAVE BEEN DOING A TREMENDOUS AMOUNT of work to rid yourself of your depression and to feel better about yourself and your world. In Chapter 18, I began discussing the one-step-at-a-time concept, making incremental changes to be efficient and to avoid putting too much pressure on yourself in the process. Making your changes slowly allows your brain to adjust and learn new ways of doing things, and as a result, your life can begin to improve.

Making all the changes and applying them as larger movements forward would be an overwhelming task. Your depression will never allow that, and that would be an unreasonable request. We have talked about going slow and taking small steps. That is exactly how we will approach applying your new changes. As you make those little incremental movements forward, I'm going to help you learn to apply each step before you move to the next one.

In Chapter 18, I presented The 8 Steps of Change. Number eight on that list is, *When you feel confident that you were able to make that small change, you will discuss the next change step in detail with your counselor until you understand what is involved, and are ready to implement the steps necessary to facilitate the next change.* Also, in Chapter 20, I gave you the 10 Steps of Incremental Forward Movement. Number ten on that list is *Discuss your progress, and move to the next step in the change when you are ready.* It's so important that you understand what you did, and how it leads into the next step you are going to take. Discuss what you did with your counselor, and what is involved in the next step you are going to take.

So, to summarize, after you have prioritized the incremental step for change you are going to start with, you discuss it with your counselor, implement the plan, and when you and your counselor are sure that you have worked through that step, you begin to define the next step. When this is done, as you did with the first step, you begin the next step.

Remember to take things slowly and consistently to avoid becoming overwhelmed. It is important to keep moving forward, but that does not mean you have to be uncomfortable to the point that you give up on the program. Since I do not want you to discuss too many of those little incremental steps without applying them, it is important to understand how to work through the steps in your counseling format and apply them in your life as you are learning them. This helps to keep you from losing sight of what each little step is designed to do and helps you apply them in smaller increments. You have already prioritized steps, so you know what all of them are. You are just going slow, and taking them one step at a time. The following little step summary will help keep that actionable for you.

> **THE FIVE RULES OF LITTLE STEP APPLICATION**
>
> 1. Completely discuss the step that leads to your desired change with your counselor as your guide.
>
> 2. Discuss how to apply this step in real life with your counselor.
>
> 3. When you understand what your counselor is advising, include your advocate and other members of your support network in the process.
>
> 4. With their support, begin to apply your new change in your life.
>
> 5. Discuss your progress with your counselor routinely as you move forward in the program until you are both satisfied that enough progress has been made to move to the next little step.

KEEPING IT SMALL

Up to this point, I have presented all the necessary information you need to understand the dynamics of depression on the physical, intellectual, and emotional levels. Your support network has been there for you when you needed them and will help you identify and schedule appointments with professional practitioners, including your personal counselor.

All of this is designed to help you begin to make the changes that will free you from the clutches of the life thief to live a happy and productive life. Having discussed these changes and how to implement them with your counselor, the next logical step is to apply them in your personal life.

It is not unusual for people to try to make large changes and then apply them or to discuss small changes and wait until they feel they have made enough progress to apply several at one time. This, of course, reduces the potential success of your application process. As I began to assert in Chapter 10, it is important for you to gather and understand information about depression and how to move past it. Now, with the help of your counselor and support network, it is time to apply that information. Some of that application process will have come from what I have presented here. This information is designed to increase your knowledge base about depression so that you may use it with your counselor and other professionals.

You and your counselor have combined the relevant information with your personal experience with depression and are designing a program to meet your specific needs. That information has set the stage for the changes that are necessary in your life, and you are beginning to undertake the steps to make those changes. Now it is time to put your growth into action, and through action, you will begin to see the program come alive in your life.

As I have stated in both *The Fix Yourself Handbook* and *The Fix Your Anxiety Handbook*, knowledge alone does not create power. Gaining knowledge and learning how to apply it is the catalyst for true power. Your goal is to move away from the fearful clutches of the life thief and become a capable person, with the potential become a powerful person.

I purposely avoid giving you advice that you may apply to your own personal bout with depression. As I mentioned in Chapter 4, your depression is yours. You have your own personal life thief, and its dynamics will be based on your own individual genetics, personal experiences, and symptoms. Putting together a plan is a personal matter between you and your counselor. Together, you and your counselor will discuss your information, and together you will define and finally implement your program changes.

I want you to have all the information you need to build the foundation for your change and to understand how to open up about this debilitating condition. It is so important to let others in to help you, to eventually engage a counselor to help you through your depression, and finally to begin to live your life according to your own new personal normal, the one you are beginning create. Define the program with your counselor and begin to implement it. Once again, take this one step at a time. Just keep going. You are worth all the time it takes, and you *can* do this!

TIME TO TAKE ACTION

1. Use the 5 Rules of Little Step Application as a guide to help you implement your steps. Share them with your counselor.

2. Make sure you understand each step of the plan you and your counselor are defining together. Ask questions if you must and be clear about what you must do to begin applying what you are learning.

3. When you understand what to do in each step you will take to change your life, talk with your counselor about how to apply those little steps, one at a time.

4. Be willing to incorporate the steps you are discussing with your counselor into your personal life. Try not to be discouraged if you have a little difficulty. This is why you have a counselor.

5. Include your support network in your little step application process. They can be instrumental in giving you the support you need.

6. Journal about the changes you are making as you apply each step toward growth. Talk about your progress and any concerns you with what you are attempting to do, and don't forget to give yourself a little pat on the back for every attempt you make.

7. As you are applying the new step, discuss your progress and any difficulty you experience with your counselor, and let them help keep you consistent, focused, and moving forward.

 **DRIVING IT HOME**

This is the application stage of your program. Change is always a bit intimidating. Don't give up and try not to pull back. Expect a few challenges. They will be there, but each of them has a solution. Always remember what it is like to live in the clutches of the life thief and know that as long as you stay consistent with your treatment program, each challenge will have a solution. Discuss any concerns you have with your counselor and stay consistent—and good things can happen.

YOUR DECLARATION IS: *I will apply the changes I am making in my life one step at a time!*

 **ONWARD**

You are doing a tremendous amount of work to change your life. You may be asking yourself what these changes are leading to. It is important for you to understand what normal is in your life. In the next chapter, I am going to show you how to define your own new personal normal.

CHAPTER 22

Defining Your New Personal Normal: Understanding That You Do Belong

Understanding that you're new personal normal is the right normal for you paves the way for the belonging that can redefine your world.

PROCESSES TO EMPLOY: Brutal Honesty, I Over E, Present/Understand/Fix, Slowing Down Life's Pace, Internal Focus, Fact-Finding, Incremental Forward Movement, Boundary Setting, Faith, Trust, Internal Balance, Love

UP TO NOW, YOUR FOCUS HAS BEEN on the work you need to do to reduce depression's hold on your life. There was, and still is, much work to do with your counselor and other practitioners, and most of your attention needs to be firmly rooted in this work. Though I have strongly advised that you keep your attention focused on today and on the little steps you are taking to gain control of your life and be happy, there will always be that little part of you that wonders where all of this is going. It is not uncommon for any of us to have a plan to reach your goal, but we also like to have a good idea of what it will look like when we get there.

I began by giving you the information you needed about your depression. Working with your neurotransmitter imbalance and everything you needed to do to make your body healthy was your starting point. From there, I discussed your intellectual and emotional concerns, and we began to lay the groundwork for the treatment plan that will change your life. You know you have a personal life thief and that you need a personal treatment plan to rid yourself of its dastardly influence. With that plan in the works, you have a direction in your life, but having been at the mercy of the life thief for so long, understanding what a normal existence looks like can be difficult.

GETTING NORMAL

When depression rules your world, it is so difficult to understand what normal means. For so long, you have been a prisoner, suffocating under the thief's strangling grasp, unable to move past its clutches and define a world that makes sense to you. Depression created a norm in your life, and you lived according to that norm. You knew that living your life according to the terms dictated by the life thief was not normal, but the definition of "normal" seemed to be far out of your reach.

While in the clutches of depression, it is easy to compare yourself to those people you feel are normal and attempt to use what you believe their version of normal is as a metric in your own life. There are two problems with this:

1. You have no idea what is going on in other people's lives and if they are, in fact, living a life they feel is normal. You don't live in their skin, so it is hard to know what they think and feel. It is hard to achieve something when its parameters are so undefined.

2. Just as your depression is a personal matter for you, so is the concept of normal. Trying to internalize someone else's version of normal can be an exercise in futility since you do not share their exact genetics or their life experiences.

I will define "normal" in a way that can help you as you move forward in your program. *Normal is when your thought processes are realistic and possess clarity, when your emotions are healthy and positive, and when you can feel connected to yourself and the world you are living in.* Just as you are a unique person and you have your own personal life thief, you will be creating your own personal normal according to this definition. Everything I am teaching you is designed to help you live a healthy and normal life. All the information about depression I have been providing throughout this book is intended to give you the tools you need make this happen.

Instead of comparing yourself to anyone else, strive to create the person you want to be—your own personal normal. No one ever succeeds in trying to be someone else. There is no universal normal. Your genetics and the people and experiences in your life, as we have discussed earlier, will define who you are, and that goes a long way into helping you develop your own personal normal. However, there is a tool you can use to refine that process and to have more say in the direction of your personal normal development: conscious thought. Instead of just letting your world develop, put conscious thought into everything you are doing to get there. In *The Fix Yourself Handbook*, I discuss the concepts of autopilot, and engaging your brain in what you do. The more conscious thought you put into something, the more efficient you can be at accomplishing what you set out to do. Conscious thought helps you develop a sense of what normal is, since the changes you are making are specific to you, and you are thinking about them as you are making them.

This is why your counselor is so important in your movement forward. Your first goal was to learn everything you could about depression. You understood that your world was not normal and that you finally needed to do something about it. Acquiring the information came first, followed by all the steps to get your body healthy and start working with your emotions on the effect depression has had on the way you think and feel. Now, armed with the help of your counselor and support network, it is time you start defining your own personal normal.

> ### The 8 Steps to Define Your New Personal Normal
>
> 1. Understand that there is no universal concept of normal.
> 2. Compare your normal to no one else's normal.
> 3. Learn to understand and define how you think and feel.
> 4. Create a life plan that fits you and your needs.
> 5. Work on your plan with your counselor, step by step.
> 6. Discuss everything you are doing and how you think and feel with your counselor and your advocate.
> 7. Discuss how the gains you are making are redefining the way you think and feel.
> 8. Begin to discuss your gains in the context of your new personal normal.

To help you apply the eight steps, I'm going to explain them in greater detail. This will help you understand what I mean when I say that there is no universal normal and that you do not need to attempt to belong to a one-size-fits-all societal norm.

Understand that there is no universal concept of normal.

When we began discussing the counseling component of your treatment plan, we talked about getting all the information possible because you are unique and specific to yourself. We didn't want a cookie-cutter version of a treatment program to help you because your life thief is yours and yours alone. Your personal normal follows the same rule. What is normal for someone else has nothing to do with you. Just like the information I gave you about depression, there are general rules that apply, but to define who you are, we take the personal approach. Your normal is yours. Embracing it is all about defining it, not shaping into an imitation of another's normal.

Compare your normal to no one else's normal.

Before you began discussing who you are with your support network and your counselor, very few people understood you. This is because no one can completely understand anyone else. We can get close with the people we are intimate with, but for the most part, it is very difficult to understand how another person thinks, feels, and behaves. Attempting to imitate the normal that defines their life is an exercise in futility. You do not know them well enough, and you will never fully understand their normal. You will always come up short and feel as though you are not normal. Let their normal be theirs.

Learn to understand and define how you think and feel.

When we began incorporating the counseling component into your treatment program, the goal was to define the information you were presenting, arrange it in an actionable format, and use it to change your life. The first step in that process was to present the information, followed by identifying steps you need to take to define and understand it. We discussed journaling about this while you work with your counselor, making changes when necessary, and understanding how you think and feel along the way. *Focus your attention on understanding yourself.* This will go a long way toward defining your personal normal.

Create a life plan that fits you and your needs.

Your counselor is helping you formulate a life plan that is based on all the information you gave them. In Chapter 17, when I discussed working with a counselor, one of the most important suggestions was that you provide this person with as much information as possible so they can accurately understand how you think and feel. This allows them to help you formulate a plan to meet your personal, specific needs. You are not trying to be someone else. You are perfect the way you are, and with a few tweaks needed here and there, you can learn to understand what normal means for you.

Work on your plan with your counselor, step by step.

Attempting to be normal like everyone else is like trying to get to a destination without understanding where you are going. This is why we use a step-by-step plan. Each little step gives you more understanding about yourself, helps you define the world you live in, and helps you establish what is normal for you. Keep working the steps and talking about them with your counselor. You will define your normal there.

Discuss everything you are doing and how you think and feel about with your counselor and advocate

If you want to feel normal, you should have clear idea of what your normal is. You do this by discussing everything with your counselor. Discussing it with your support network and journaling about it further defines the program and how you feel about it. While you go through all these steps, you continue to add definition to the way you think and feel and to the world you are living in. You are going to feel comfortable in the world you're recreating, and therein lies your personal normal.

Discuss how the gains you are making are redefining the way you think and feel.

These last two steps are important. First, you are going to realize that your world is becoming redefined. The little steps you are accomplishing will lend definition to it. It is so important for you to talk about what is changing in your world and how you feel about. Talk about what changes you are making and how your thoughts and feelings are changing along with the gains you make. You are taking the first step to understanding your new personal normal.

Begin to discuss your gains in the context of your personal normal.

In this step, it is so important to focus on your normal. Here is where you begin to understand that you do not need to be the way the rest of the world wants you to be. Also, you will begin to realize that you do not have to be person the life thief wanted you to be. This is where you can give yourself permission to be the person **you** want to be.

YOU BELONG

Keep this in mind: there is no universal normal. There are societal norms, but what you think and feel is yours, and yours alone. The goal of your own personal normal is simply to help your mind function with clarity so you are happy, and so you feel you belong in this world with others. When you think about it, that is all you have ever been looking for. You have always felt that you were on the outside looking in, and no matter what you did, you just didn't fit in. The real problem was that you did not understand how to fit in with yourself. You did not grasp how important it was to understand and accept yourself so that you could begin to understand what personal normal is. Happiness is not found in trying to mimic another's normal. Rather it is understanding your own personal normal that will create the happiness you have been so desperate to experience.

Defining your new life parameters means nothing more than working with your program, staying close to your counselor and your support network, and not quitting. It means defining your own personal normal. In Chapter 1, I said that depression is not a one-size-fits-all approach and that you have your own personal life thief. Likewise, normal is not a one-size-fits-all definition. You have the right to establish what "normal" personally means to you. So, as you are coming to the end of this book, embrace the information and the steps I have provided you with and work with your counselor and your support network to build that beautiful world where you can be free of the life thief, where you can be your own personal normal and say, "I am happy, and I belong." You are beautiful, and you *do* belong.

 **TIME TO TAKE ACTION**

1. Discuss the concept of your own personal normal with your counselor. This will help you gain more insights into the directions you might take as your counseling continues.

2. Keep your focus on your own normal and no one else's. Remember, there is no one-size-fits-all in normal, and the right version of normal for you is your own.

3. Use the the 8 Steps to Define Your New Personal Normal. Discuss them with your counselor and also with your support network.

4. Journal about the steps you are taking to define what normal is for you. Include your thoughts and feelings and discuss them routinely with your counselor.

5. Approach your treatment plan and your life with the understanding that you are worthy and you do belong. This will help you approach the changes you are making in your life with the positive attitude you need.

 DRIVING IT HOME

Before you began working your counselor, the life thief had you convinced that you were different and that nothing would change. You compared yourself with other people you felt were happier than you, convinced that they were normal and you were not.

Beginning to define your own personal normal is a key component in the plan to free yourself from the clutches of the life thief. It is always nice to have an idea of where you are going. This helps pave the way for the steps you will take to make your program a successful one. Your counselor, skilled in the techniques of bringing you through your depression, will have an idea of what normal looks like. Begin talking that over with your counselor and make that a goal you both understand. Commit and remain motivated to reaching your personal normal.

YOUR DECLARATION IS: *I will define my normal. I will live with clarity and happiness, and I will belong.*

 **ONWARD**

As we come to the last chapter of this book, I will close with the same commentary with which I close all of my programs: You are doing what you can to change your life, and if you stay with the program and your counselor, change will happen, and in time, you can begin to feel better. However, from time to time, old foes can make a reappearance. In this last chapter, I will show you how to deal with that little life thief when it tries to make its way back into your life.

CHAPTER 23

Good Housekeeping: Keeping Order in Your New World

Life thieves, large and small, love to make return visits. You banished them the first time, and you can do it again.

PROCESSES TO EMPLOY: Brutal Honesty, I Over E, Present/Understand/Fix, Slowing Down Life's Pace, Internal Focus, Fact-Finding, System Maintenance, Housekeeping

---

YOU ARE TO BE CONGRATULATED for the attempts you are making to send the life thief packing and to begin introducing the productivity and happiness you deserve into your life. The correct knowledge about depression and the hard work you are doing are the prescription for success, and if you stay committed, your life can change. For all of us, when we do hard work and begin to realize the fruits of our labors, we firmly believe that those well-deserved changes we are making should be permanent. Why would we think otherwise?

You have decided to make changes in your life, and you have stayed committed to the work you need to do to make that happen. It is critical that you are protective of them. At times, you may experience brief periods when you regress a bit or reinvolve yourself in some old, bad habits.

When I counsel people, they often assume they have taken a step backward when this occurs. When this happens, you can lose your focus. When those productive plans that are helping you move forward seem compromised, you can experience some of those old negative feelings. This can cause you to question whether you are really capable of making the changes that are so important to you. Your life is a fluid and dynamic enterprise; it will continue to change, and the good and not-so-good will routinely enter your life.

ENTITLED, NO; EFFICIENT, YES

Just because you did the work to make yourself healthier, wiser, and stronger does not mean that the life-stealing monster will not try to find its way back into your life. Life does not stop just because you made some improvements; it is an ongoing affair, and the challenges inherent in living in an ever-changing world will continuously appear. It would be foolish to assume otherwise. This life is fluid and ongoing and absolutely loaded with wonderful people and events. At the same time, it is infested with little toxins and demons we would like to strangle, especially when they make return visits. Sometimes, intellectual and emotional housekeeping is in order.

When this happens, the formula is to, once again, assess the situation, understand where you went wrong, and continue working with the program I have been outlining for you, with the assistance of your counselor and your support network. You are not perfect. You are going to have lapses in judgment, and at times, you are going to regress to some of your previous behaviors. There will be times when you just got tired and made a mistake.

There may be some negative energy involved in your actions, but that does not mean you are not making progress or that this negative energy is guaranteed to continue moving forward with you as your life continues. All of us make mistakes, and it makes good sense to address the errors we make quickly. Doing so allows us to return to what works for us and to the positive energy that exists there.

Especially in the initial stages of the changes you are making, there will be a bit of back and forth movement as you make progress and then regress a bit. Remember, you are retraining your brain. This, as I have stated several times, is a function of repetition over time. So, when you think you have done the work and your depression should be either reduced or alleviated altogether, remember that the condition is based on neurochemical imbalance. At times, things may run smoothly, while at other times there may be challenges. This is to be expected, so try not to get overwhelmed when it happens.

YOU GOT THIS

Keep this in mind: You were paralyzed by the effects of your life thief. Your circumstances ranged from depressed but manageable to completely dysfunctional. With the help of the information you received in this book and from your counselor and support network, you began to make changes, and as a result, you began to feel better.

You dealt with depression on that level, and things are looking up. What would make you think you do not have the skills to do it again? Now that you are armed with a support network, a counselor, and so many other professionals, every battle you wage with your life thief involves reinforcements to help you put that little monster back where it belongs—out of your life.

Every so often, you are going to need to do a little house cleaning. Every now and then, you have to pick up that little life thief by the seat of its pants and kick it out of your world. You are not alone anymore. You have your people. Use them same way you did to start the whole process. Here is one of those little refrigerator reminders that could help you when the life thief is peeking around the corner.

> **THE SEVEN STEPS FOR SUCCESSFUL HOUSECLEANING**
>
> 1. Be ready for a return visit; it is coming.
> 2. Identify the intruder's return visit.
> 3. Be honest about what you are experiencing.
> 4. Slow down and keep your emotions in check.
> 5. Gather all the necessary facts and discuss them with your counselor. Do this quickly!
> 6. Based on the facts, develop a plan to address the problem.
> 7. Execute your plan completely and stay close to your counselor and your support network.

Never forget that you are beautiful and worthy. You have all the right in the world to be happy and live your life as a productive and capable person. Once again, depression is not who you are; it is a condition you have. With the right information, the right professionals, and your support network available to you, depression is a beatable condition. Stay committed, and never give up. Stay close to your support network and your counselor. Never see yourself as anything but a beautiful, wonderful, and loving person—because that is who you are. The world is waiting for you with open arms. Let them love you, and you will learn to love yourself.

⏱ Time to Take Action

1. Always remember that depression is a beatable condition. Stay close to your support network and your counselor. Bring them into every aspect of your life.

2. There will be bumps and challenges along the way. Some of them will not be so little. You are not alone anymore. Do not let the life thief isolate you again. Use your support network to help you fight back, and always keep yourself open to them.

3. Return visits from depression do not mean you have slipped backward. Often, they mean you are unearthing new ground and that a little more has to be addressed. That is why you have a counselor and a support network. Never forget them.

4. Remember the little steps. Make slow, consistent progress, and never stop. There is no life to be lived in the rearview mirror, so don't look back. Just keep yourself focused on where you are going, one step at a time.

5. Talk to yourself kindly. Always give yourself credit for what you do.

6. There are no failures in this program. There are challenges, and every challenge has a solution. Never forget that.

7. Be grateful for as much as you can, have faith in yourself, and, if possible, lean on your higher power. Let others love you and begin to build a world that you like. Loving yourself starts there.

🎱 Driving It Home

Removing the life thief from your life is a tall order, but you have begun to see your depression as a beatable condition. Success comes to people who never quit, who firmly believe they are worthy of a positive and loving life, and who are unwilling to give up. Stay away from the life thief's isolating prison, open your mind and your heart to your support network and your counselor, and become the person you were meant to be. Always remember that you are a beautiful person who is worthy of everything good life has to offer. Be beautiful! Stay beautiful!

YOUR DECLARATION IS: *This is my life, and I am going to be happy!*

ONWARD!

Conclusion

When you started reading this book, you were controlled by depression, and it looked like you had no way out of your dark, unmotivated world. As you began reading this book, many of the myths surrounding depression began to fall by the wayside. Now you have an abundance of accurate information to define the nature of this debilitating condition, which helps you to understand this condition and how it affects your life.

As you continued to page through this book, you began to seize informed control of your world, and you realized that depression is *not* who you are. It is not a lifelong prison sentence that will never end or change. It does not have to continue to beat you down one day after another. There is a logical way out of your distress. Depression does not define you. It is a condition you have, and there are practical ways to address it. You are who you are. All you needed to do was to understand that, and champion who you are.

With the help of a network of trusted people to support you, practitioners who understand depression and can help you deal with its physical and emotional effects, and a personal counselor as your confidant and guide through this condition, you can see the light at the end of depression's deep, dark tunnel. Every problem has a solution, and depression is no exception.

Never forget that you are a good person who is worthy of all the good things life has to offer. Pay close attention to the information in this book and use your support network every day. Let your primary care physician be your personal program quarterback, and use all the resources from other practitioners that are available to you.

Develop an intimate relationship with your counselor, and let that person guide you through all the new experiences that are waiting for you. Stay close to your support network. There's a wonderful life waiting for you. Be willing to do the work, and remember that you are no longer alone and at the mercy of the life thief. Build the world you like, let others love you, and learn to love yourself. It's your time! Let nothing stop you!

References

Ruggiero, Faust, M.S. *The Fix Yourself Handbook*. Bangor, Pa. FYHB Publications, 2019.

Ruggiero, Faust, M.S. *The Fix Your Anxiety Handbook*. Bangor, Pa. FYHB Publications, 2023.

About the Author

Faust A. Ruggiero's professional career spans over forty years of diversified, cutting-edge counseling programs in pursuit of professional excellence and personal life enhancement. He is a published research author, clinical trainer, and a therapist with experience in clinics for deaf children, prisons, nursing homes, substance abuse centers, inpatient facilities, and major national and international corporations. He has served as the president of the Community Psychological Center in Bangor, Pennsylvania, in which capacity he developed the Process Way of Life counseling program, later presented as a formal text in the *Fix Yourself Handbook*.

Upon graduating from Mansfield University in 1977, he enrolled in the graduate psychology program at Illinois State University with a dual major in clinical and developmental psychology and a minor in research. He assisted in the publication of several research articles, including his thesis, "The effects of prosocial and antisocial television programs on the cognitions of children."

Upon leaving graduate school in 1979, Mr. Ruggiero worked with Antoinette Goffredo to provide counseling services and psychological intervention to adolescent deaf children. He worked with Ms. Goffredo to develop a behavioral-management program for profoundly deaf children with residual hearing.

In 1982, he accepted a position with the Lehigh Valley Alcohol Counseling Center. There, he provided individual counseling services to clientele suffering from alcohol abuse and addiction, including the twelve-step recovery process and family and intervention services. There, Mr. Ruggiero developed a Phase 2 counseling program for individuals convicted of drunk-driving offenses.

In 1984, he accepted a treatment position at Northampton County prison, where he provided psychological and substance abuse intake and counseling services to inmates. He coordinated all substance abuse and program development services for inmates. In 1986, he obtained his certification in substance abuse treatment in the state of Pennsylvania.

In 1989, Mr. Ruggiero left Northampton County prison to pursue his endeavors at the Community Psychological Center full time. As president of the Community Psychological Center, Mr. Ruggiero continued to provide services to individuals, families, those suffering with substance abuse, abused women and women in transition, as well as couples and marriage counseling, and counseling for veterans, law enforcement, and other first responders. In 1990, he began providing employees assistance programs to corporations in the state of Pennsylvania. Since then, he has been nationally and internationally recognized for his business approaches focused on strengthening corporate administrators and their workforces. In 1994, Mr. Ruggiero accepted an invitation to become a trainer for the Department of Health in Pennsylvania.

Following several years of experimentation with various therapeutic approaches that could be applied to clients individually and in families, social relationships, and business and corporate settings, Mr. Ruggiero developed and employed the Process Way of Life Counseling Program. The program consists of over fifty internal human processes, which can be accessed and developed to help clients address the various conditions affecting their lives. The program was developed, rigorously researched and tested, and revised into the approach presently being used at the Community Psychological Center.

In the summer of 2016, Mr. Ruggiero began to develop a series of books based on the Process Life Program to help readers address the difficult situations in their lives. *The Fix Yourself Handbook* was completed in December 2019 and received the Silver Award from The Nonfiction Authors Association on February 1, 2020, the Gold Award from Literary Titan on May 2, 2020, and the Bronze Award from Reader's Favorite on September , 2020. He has appeared on television, radio shows, and podcasts both national and international to discuss the Process Way of Life presented in *The Fix Yourself Handbook*. His radio show "Fix It With Faust" debuted in June 2021. On June 8, 2023, the second installment in The Fix Yourself Empowerment Series, *The Fix Your Anxiety Handbook*, was published. It is also an award-winning publication. In December, 2003, *The Fix Your Depression Handbook* was published. It is the third book in The Fix it Yourself Empowerment Series.

www.ingramcontent.com/pod-product-compliance
Lightning Source LLC
Chambersburg PA
CBHW072154070526
44585CB00015B/1130